Nathan Brown

The history of Magnus Maharba and the Black Dragon

Nathan Brown

The history of Magnus Maharba and the Black Dragon

ISBN/EAN: 9783744739122

Printed in Europe, USA, Canada, Australia, Japan

Cover: Foto ©ninafisch / pixelio.de

More available books at **www.hansebooks.com**

THE HISTORY

OF

MAGNUS MAHARBA

AND THE

BLACK DRAGON.

BY

KRISTOFUR KADMUS.

From the Original Manuscripts.

NEW-YORK:
PRINTED FOR THE PROPRIETOR.
1867.

PUBLISHERS' NOTE.

SOME time since certain curious manuscripts were discovered in the library of a New York antiquarian, purporting to be chapters in the history of a king named Magnus Maharba. The orthography was quite unlike any thing known to the present generation, and bore a strong resemblance to the old Saxon, every sound having its appropriate character, while the silent letters, introduced into our language by the Norman French, were wholly wanting.

This remarkable story has been published and widely circulated in its original form, but many persons find a difficulty in reading it, on account of its antique spelling. The present edition will obviate that objection.

The author of the work gives no clew to the time or place of the occurrences he has narrated. The publishers have a suspicion that it is not as ancient as it would at first seem; but they will leave the reader to form his own opinion after completing the story.

The work, in its original Saxon-like orthography, may be obtained of the publishers, Brown and Duer, New-York city.

CONTENTS.

		PAEG
I.	ORIGIN OF THE BLACK DRAGON	5
II.	SAMUNCLE AND HIS DAUGHTER FREDEEMA	11
III.	FREDEEMA BECOMES A WANDERER	16
IV.	OSSAMIE DIES FOR FREDEEMA	22
V.	CORONATION OF MAGNUS MAHARBA	30
VI.	COMMENCEMENT OF THE DRAGONIAN WAR	35
VII.	BLOODY BATTLES IN VIRGINLAND	41
VIII.	SAMUNCLE PLEADS FOR FREDEEMA	48
IX.	DRAGONIAN INVASION OF NORLAND	53
X.	PAINFUL SUSPENSE OF FREDEEMA	59
XI.	LIBERATION OF THE KUSHANS	66
XII.	OPENING OF THE FATHERWATER	71
XIII.	SECOND INVASION OF NORLAND	77
XIV.	DIABOLIAN METHODS OF WARFARE	85
XV.	TRIUMPH OF THE FREDONIAN ARMS	92
XVI.	MARTYRDOM OF MAGNUS MAHARBA	99

MAGNUS MAHARBA.

CHAPTER I.

ORIGIN OF THE BLACK DRAGON.

SMALL PLANET in one of the starry clusters on the outer margin of the universe was the scene of the transactions recorded in the following pages. They occurred about six thousand years after that orb began to be peopled with rational intelligences. The exact period, according to their reckoning, when the Black Dragon commenced his war upon the good king Magnus Maharba, was A. M. VDCCCLXI. Now A. M. is their abbreviation for Anno Manni, or Anno Mundi, signifying year of the man-world. For the inhabitants suppose their world to have been made out of the ruins of some former world, judging from the remains of hideous reptiles, enormous frogs, lizards, dragons, and other monsters which they have found imbedded in the rocks, swamps, and alluvial deposits. There are at present on the planet a class of monomaniacs, called geologists, who spend their lives in digging up and assorting those disagreeable creatures, and calculating the periods of antiquity in which they respectively flourished. For the amusement of young

people, these amiable enthusiasts publish curious books filled with outlandish pictures of the various goblin forms that crawled, crept, swam, or soared, among the confused and warring elements, in the foggy dawn of creation.

Whether the Black Dragon was one of the original prehuman inhabitants, who by a remarkable tenacity of life had survived the revolutions that swept all the other primeval occupants into chaos, or whether he was a mushroom production of later date which it would be right to exterminate, was a point much disputed. The most learned men were divided; but a majority of the lawyers and spiritual doctors were of opinion that the Black Dragon belonged to the primitive formations; or that he was at least coeval in his origin with man, and should be treated with due respect as a good creature of God, and a joint proprietor of the planetary domain.

The globe of which I write, notwithstanding its inferiority in size, was one of the most beautiful in the whole circle of the heavens. Its soil was rich, its fruits delicious, its flowers exquisitely tasteful, and its airs redolent with perfumes. But the men were of a bad race, — selfish, passionate, quarrelsome, and worshipers of a great number of idol gods. It has been asserted that their nature, soon after it came from the hands of the Creator, received a taint from the breath of a snaky apparition that insinuated itself into the arbor of the first pair, and whose poison has contaminated all their offspring. Learned scholars and antiquarians, who have thoroughly investigated the subject, think there can be no doubt that the Black Dragon is a direct descendant of that same old serpent who injected his deadly venom into the venis of their progenitors.

The orb on which man and the Dragon dwelt had two large islands, one on either side, which were called, in the language of that sphere, the Great Orient and the Great Occident. There were also very wide oceans between them. And the Great Orient was the larger of the two islands, for it extended lengthwise quite across one side of the planet, and its north-western and south-western extremities, called Nora and Kusha, stretched far out into the sea. During the first five thousand years of man, the Great Occident was scarcely known to the dwellers in the Orient, and even the dim tradition that such an island existed was at length forgotten. But once upon a time an adventurous sea-captain, named Christopher, sailing westward, chanced to discover it. He found it peopled by strange races, who were seized with terror at his approach, thinking the new-comers had descended from the skies. When Christopher returned to his own country, and described the beauty of the land he had found, and told of the gold and silver and diamonds with which it abounded, the report quickly spread through cities and provinces, and all the people were filled with wonder. And they began to come out in swarms, like bees from a hundred hives, thinking to better their condition by removing to a country that was so rich. And they poured over in ships and galleys, and took possession of the Great Occident, establishing their colonies in the south, and in the north, and in the centre.

Meanwhile the Black Dragon, by some diabolical instinct, perceived the growing greatness of the young colonies in the land of gold, and he said to himself, Shall the race of man enjoy this new paradise alone, and I have no part therein? So he formed his plan, and on the evening of a stormy day he mounted a whirlwind and dashed off upon the waters, puffing and snorting like a steam-engine. And he had several ships that accompanied him, to supply him with food and necessaries during his voyage. Day after day he swept on, now soaring aloft over the mountain waves, now plunging beneath the surface and shooting through the blue waters, like a Norwegian kraken. Mermen and mermaids, whales, sea-serpents, and all the finny tribes shrunk from his approach, and hid themselves in their ocean caverns while he passed by. About a month had elapsed when, in the dubious light of a misty morning, his dark scaly form was descried emerging from the waves and crawling up on the sandy beach of the Occident. There he languidly rolled himself about, surveying with bloated and fiery eyes the regions around, and quietly devouring every thing that came in his way. It was afterwards discovered that on the bottom of the ocean, all along the line of his track, there was piled up a great highway of whitened bones, the skeletons of human victims that had been killed and eaten by him on his passage from one island to the other.

No sooner was the Black Dragon fairly settled upon the Occident coast than he began to gather around him great numbers of people, whom he allured with the promise of vast riches, ease from labor, and joint dominion of all that portion of the great island which was called Sunland. These friends and allies of his were called Dragonians, after the name of their patron. By their assistance he fitted out swift ships and sent them across the ocean, to the land of the Kushans, there to buy, steal, and capture strong men and young women, healthy boys and fair damsels, and bring them over to become menials and helots, and to till the fields, and to prepare soft raiment for himself and his servants. And the country became full of people, and the nobles grew wealthy and proud, like the lords of the old kingdoms whence they came.

Now there were but few laws in Sunland, and none were considered absolutely binding except the laws for holding fast the Kushans and killing off a sufficient number of them every year to feed the Black Dragon. For the Dragon was a voracious eater, albeit he was very dainty, and did not relish the flesh of his victims unless it had been well bruised and flagellated to make it tender and savory. The Dragonians, understanding this, commenced the mangling of the young Kushans at a very early age, and by a slow process of torture made their flesh exceedingly delicate and palatable. It was a great art to find out how best to prolong the lives of these unhappy creatures while undergoing the rigorous treatment to which they were subjected. The Dragon had a professional class called Overlookers, who made that study their special business. To gratify their prince they invented many curious engines for lacerating and mangling the flesh of the helots; and divers iron rings and fetters of iron; also stocks for their hands and feet, and gags of iron for their mouths; and wonderful burning mixtures to pour upon their bodies after cutting and tearing the skin with whips and saws and perforated wooden mauls.

This foul monster also practiced the horrible rite of miscegenation; for whenever he saw among the Kushans any beautiful young women, whether wives or maidens, he ordered them to be brought before him, and they were forced to become his wives, for they knew that if they should oppose his wishes he would tear them limb from limb.

The Black Dragon, notwithstanding his brutish deformities, was a great favorite with people of rank and fashion. He kept a magnificent court, and had a splendid retinue. His servants practiced a great variety of arts to render his appearance comely. His horns were concealed by the crown and jewels with which he was ornamented. His face was seemingly human, except when he attempted to smile, and then his grinning and misshapen teeth gave such a savage expression to his countenance that his friends and admirers would frequently start back with terror. His huge and scaly carcass was enveloped in robes of velvet and silk; and as he sat upon his ebon throne, his attendants, with their showy trains, were ranged around him in such a way as to hide his long tail from the view of visitors. Fair ladies and gallant knights thronged his palace, and were loud in praise of the glory and greatness of their prince, who, they imagined, would one day become the ruler of the world.

CHAPTER II.

SAMUNCLE AND HIS DAUGHTER FREDEEMA.

ESIDES the Black Dragon there were other longevians who did not belong to the race of men, and whose lives were not limited, like theirs, to a hundred revolutions of the planet, but who remained age after age, and exerted a powerful influence on passing generations. In the common dialect of the inhabitants these old residents were called by such names as seemed most expressive of their respective characters. One of them, a wrinkled and repulsive antediluvian, was called Tyranny; another, a female, of somewhat milder countenance and more polite demeanor, was known as Monarchia; and there was a wild, crazy bacchanal, worse than Tyranny himself, who went by the name of Anarchia.

While some of these longevians were malevolent beings, the offspring of the infernals, who delighted only in misery and ruin, others were of celestial birth, and all their intercourse with mortals was kind and happy; they appeared to have no desire but to bring back mankind to their original truth and virtue. There were also on the same planet giants, or demi-gods, who partook of both natures, the celestial and the mortal; combining the power and influence of the one with the infirmities and errors of the other.

It was several hundred years after the time of Christopher that a young giant by the name of Samuncle began to be famous in the country of the Occidentals. He was of celestial parentage, being a descendant of Friga, the Goddess of Liberty. His eldest daughter, Fredeema, was a lovely creature, whose extraordinary beauty, even in infancy, enchanted all beholders. As she grew up, her fame spread through the island, and across the sea, and to the most distant lands. And the Black Dragon fixed his eyes upon her, and when he saw her beauty he determined to make her his bride.

Samuncle was the most extensive land-holder on the western island, and he finally became possessor of all those rich tracts known as the United Occident. In order to encourage laborers to settle on his lands he allowed the cultivators to occupy them without rent, supporting himself on the princely revenues that he was able to accumulate by trade with foreign nations. It was understood, however, that in case of war, or other emergency, the occupants of the soil should bear the necessary burdens of the country.

But the kings in some of the Noran countries were displeased at the liberality of Samuncle. For they said, It is not good that the people should be relieved from their rents; this example will work mischief, and will spread discontent among our subjects. And the king of Bullia spake to Monarchia, the goddess whom he worshiped, and she bade him send over and collect the rents himself. For, said she, those people went out from your own kingdom, and therefore they are your subjects still. So he sent over his messengers and his tax-gatherers, as she advised him. But the people refused their demands, and declared they would pay no rent, tribute, or custom to the king of the Bullians. Then he sent over his armies to contend with them in battle, and to vanquish and subdue them. But they met with disaster, and could not accomplish the king's desire.

And Samuncle summoned the chiefs and heads of the people to a great council. And they obeyed the call, and hasted and came together, in full numbers, and sat in council many days. And they said, We will cast off the king's yoke, and make us kings of our own; and Monarchia shall be deposed from her queenly dignity throughout the entire Occident; and in her stead we will choose the gentle Fredeema, and crown her perpetual queen, and she shall be the goddess around whose tri-colored banner we will rally our warriors. So they communed with her father, and appointed a day when he should bring her out to them, that they might do her homage. And on the fourth day of the month Julius she came before them with blushing countenance and leaning on her father's arm; and they crowned her with a golden crown, and led her forth before all the people, and the people shouted and clapped their hands, and cried, Fredeema forever! And the council ordained that the anniversary of that day should ever after be kept as a holiday, and be called Coronation Day; and that all their kings should take an oath to protect, defend, and preserve the honor and supremacy of Fredeema, and that whoever conspired against her should suffer death.

But alas! the hour of triumph is often the hour of peril, and this the gentle Fredeema afterward learned to her sorrow. In the council that showed her such honors there were messengers from Sunland, who were Dragonians; but they made no claim in behalf of their prince that he should share in the government of the country. On their return home the Dragon chid them because they had been unmindful of his interests, and had not even mentioned his name. So when the next great council was called he concluded to present himself, along with his delegates, and claim his seat as one of the chief proprietary lords and rightful occupants of the western island. But the Normen were loath to admit him to a council of humans; they, however, allowed him to speak and present his claims. He offered to join with them in forming a grand league and covenant, and to place all his forces, with those of Samuncle, at the disposal of the kings who should be chosen to rule the country, for mutual protection and defense. But he would consent to a union only on certain conditions. The object of the wily old demon was to obtain possession of Fredeema. He proposed that if they would give her to him in marriage, he would divorce his former spouse Monarchia, to whom he had been so long united in the Oriental kingdoms, and Fredeema should be his legally and honorably wedded wife, so long as rivers ran or ocean rolled.

After this they had long consultations and much debate, before they could frame the great covenant which was to be the perpetual law of the realm. The Dragonians desired that it should contain an act of betrothal binding their master and Fredeema in an indissoluble union. Samuncle and the Normen were shocked at this proposal; and yet they were so desirous of the Dragon's assistance in their wars against Monarchia that they did not dare to say nay. They therefore allowed the covenant to be written obscurely, so as to be capable of different interpretations; and to this day the meaning of some parts is disputed. It appears, however, to have been generally admitted that the instrument gave the Black Dragon a right to participate in the government, and that the framers contemplated a union between him and Fredeema. They probably hoped that he would change his nature, or at least his habits, as one of the articles provided that he should, after a short period, discontinue his traffic with the Kushan-sellers, and bring no more unhappy victims across the waters.

How it happened that the shrewd Samuncle should have given his consent to this unnatural alliance has ever been a mystery. By some it is said that he did not understand the nature and import of the covenant formed; by others, that he must have been partially insane, or perhaps stupefied with intoxicating drugs; others still maintain that he was bribed by the great advantages to be derived from a league with the Dragon. However this may be, it is plain he was never heartily in favor of the alliance; and as time rolled on, the prospect of giving up his daughter to the embrace of a monster so preyed upon his spirits that his brow was furrowed with premature wrinkles. As for the child, she would start with horror whenever the contemplated union was alluded to, and burying her face in her hands immediately rush out of sight.

CHAPTER III.

FREDEEMA BECOMES A WANDERER.

REDEEMA, being of the longevian race, did not grow up to womanhood rapidly like mortals. Her youth extended through the reigns of several of the early kings, with whom she was a great favorite. They were careful to make no allusion to her unhappy betrothal, probably hoping that the Dragon would die before the nuptials should be consummated. Annually, on coronation day, the damsel, with her maidens dressed in white, appeared before the people, and marched to the temple of Liberty, amid the acclamations of the multitudes, who strewed her path with roses, and whose admiration of her loving nature and gentle disposition had no bounds.

But this holiday was an offense to the Black Dragon, who, as oft as it returned, sat moody and unsocial in his palace, meditating on the means by which he might bring his future bride into proper subjection, and punish the Fredonians, who were fostering her vanity by their praises, and who, he shrewdly suspected, were bent on breaking up the match and snatching from his possession the object of his desire.

The Dragon was accustomed to notch every coronation day upon his spear-handle. After he had made half a hundred notches, he began to urge upon the reigning king his claim for Fredeema, demanding that she should at least be placed under restraint, and instead of wandering about at her pleasure, be committed to the guardianship of tutors who would train her to docility and submission, and would teach her, above all things else, that the Black Dragon was to be her master. The king who governed at that time would not listen to the proposal; but his reign was short, and the kings who followed him were more favorable to the Dragon, and promised him that he should have all he asked. Then the scaly old monster, finding that he had the kings upon his side, began to show out more and more of his detestable nature. He commenced making occasional visits to the house of Samuncle, frightening poor Fredeema almost to distraction, eying her with a malicious leer and showing her his horrid teeth. On one or two occasions he seized her by the hair of her head, and would have dragged her off without mercy to his own home, but for the outcry raised by the neighbors and townsfolk, who loved Fredeema as they loved their own lives.

And now the Dragon turned his vengeance upon these kind-hearted people; for when any of them ventured within his boundaries he would cause them to be apprehended and placed upon the rack, in order to ascertain whether they had any acquaintance with Fredeema; and if they betrayed the least sympathy with her or her friends the torture was continued until they died. Sometimes they were plunged under water and held there until half suffocated; then raised and plunged again, and this repeated so as to make them suffer the pangs of a dozen deaths.; sometimes they were confined in loathsome dungeons till they wasted away with hunger and disease; but the favorite mode of destroying them was by hanging them up quietly on the nearest tree. This hanging of the Fredonians went on until all Sunland was filled with the horrible and pestilential stench of decaying corpses. Travelers, when they saw the bodies suspended upon trees along the road-side, would often turn back, resolving never to attempt a journey to that country again. But the Dragon was well pleased at the slaughter of the Fredonians, and he snuffed up the fetid air as if it were the sweet-smelling odor of a burnt-sacrifice. He also told his ministers privately that when he had brought home his northern bride he would take her out daily in his carriage to view her gibbeted friends, and he would let her know that if she made any remonstrance she should share the same fate.

Reports of these horrors reached the ears of Fredeema, and made her cling the closer to her northern home. Several Kushan women who had escaped the torture of the Black Dragon found their way to her father's house, bringing their infants with them. From them she learnt the whole story of the Dragon's cruelties. Her tender heart was ready to burst, and she clasped the little Kushan babes to her bosom, showering upon them tears and kisses. She proposed to her father that he should start on a crusade against the Black Dragon, storm his castle, and kill him if necessary for the release of the captives. Young and delicate as she was, she offered to accompany him on this desperate expedition. But her father chided her for her forwardness, and told her that she would not only bring herself into trouble but him also; that the Black Dragon was the most powerful prince in the land, and next to the king himself. He told her also that he was already in fear of his life, because he had not given her in marriage when demanded. Then Fredeema trembled from head to foot, and her cheeks and lips grew white with suppressed emotion; for she saw that her father, with all his power and greatness, had no strength or courage to resist any demand which the Black Dragon might make, and that he would probably, if driven to extremity, sacrifice even a daughter to save his own life. So she ceased to urge him, but inwardly resolved that whatever might happen she would cast her lot with the poor Kushans, and that they should henceforth be her people.

The friends and neighbors now showed their strong sympathy for Fredeema, and some of them boldly pronounced it a shame that the great Samuncle should act so cowardly a part. But the gold-worshipers, and the wise men of the law, and the soul-doctors on whose judgment he relied, advised him to be cautious, and endeavor to restrain his impetuous child, and on no account allow any more Kushans to enter his house. Finding his daughter fixed in her purpose, he began to grow more and more uneasy, for he was resolved not to give her up against her will. He therefore devised various expedients to secrete and protect her; but the king of the Occident and the great judges of the kingdom, who were in accord with the Dragon, decided that the princess must be given up, according to the bond of betrothal which her father confessed that he had signed. It was not long before news came that messengers from the Black Dragon were already on their way to secure Fredeema and convey her to the abode of her acknowledged master. Her father had now no resource left but to send her away secretly. With a heavy heart he called his family together for a hasty farewell, and told his weeping daughter that he could protect her no longer; that she must now fly for her life, throwing herself on the providence of God and such assistance as the kind-hearted people might render her by the way. So when they had all embraced and kissed her, and had put into her hands a few necessaries for her journey, she started forth on her perilous pilgrimage, trusting in a watchful Providence to guide her way, but with heart palpitating at every step, for fear the emissaries of the Dragon might be upon her track.

The messengers, failing to discover her retreat, now returned home and related to the Dragon all their adventures, and the manner in which Fredeema had escaped. He was furious in his rage at the maiden for her obstinacy; and the information that she had been abandoned by her natural protector, and had no home but the caves and the forests, seemed to furnish him the stimulus of a new activity for the apprehension of his victim. He forthwith determined to search every nook and corner where the panting fugitive might have found shelter. So calling together the lords and ladies of his court, his fiery eye-balls all the while glowing with excitement, he swore a damnable oath that since Fredeema had deliberately and scornfully rejected him, he also discarded and rejected her, but would have his will upon her, and would put her to the hardest menial labor, until her plump and rosy form should be wasted to the very bones ; and then for a warning he would throw out her skeleton to whiten in the open field, along with the carcasses of the Kushans and Fredonians that were rotting in the sun and bleaching in the dews and rains of heaven. A clangor of applause, like the cheers of pandemonium, rang through the palace as he uttered this horrid oath.

And now commenced the grand hunt for the innocent and hapless Fredeema. A thousand horsemen, mounted upon fleet steeds, with blood-hounds in their train, were started off to scour the mountains and vales of Norland. Through summer and winter, in spring-time and harvest, the tramp of their steeds and the howling of their dogs sent terror to the hearts of the peaceful inhabitants. Fredeema was never safe, though the kind peasants did all they could to protect her. But she thought not of herself alone. Daily and nightly she sought out the poor Kushans who were flying from their tormentors, directing them to the houses and villages where she had been befriended, and carefully pointing out to them the polar star, by following which they would reach Snowland, a bitterly cold country, inaccessible to the Kushan hunters.

CHAPTER IV.

OSSAMIE DIES FOR FREDEEMA.

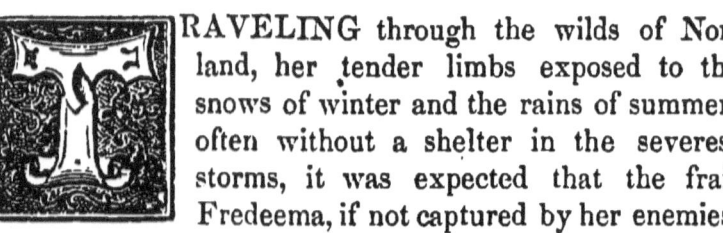RAVELING through the wilds of Norland, her tender limbs exposed to the snows of winter and the rains of summer, often without a shelter in the severest storms, it was expected that the frail Fredeema, if not captured by her enemies, would at length sink under the hardships she had to endure. But to the amazement of all, the more severe her exposure and sufferings, the stronger and healthier she grew, and so lovely in form and feature that the people all pronounced her a goddess endowed with immortality. Many also, hearing her noble words in behalf of the despised Kushans, declared themselves ready to follow her, even to the Dragon's castle, for the purpose of rescuing his miserable captives.

The Dragonians, seeing how the princess had gained the affections of the multitudes, applied to the king for a law to punish with death all who should harbor or conceal her. Then the king brought the matter before the great council, and it was agreed that the whole country should join in the search after Fredeema, and whoever refused to point out her hiding-places, or to assist in apprehending her, should be severely punished.

She was now reduced to the greatest straits; all feared to give her a night's lodging, or a crumb of bread.

In her extremity, she wandered far out into the great wilderness of the west, and finding a log-cabin, sat down before it in a state of complete exhaustion. It was occupied by an old man, whose name was Ossamie, the father of six sons. He was of a stern countenance, and had a rough, grisly beard; and when he came out to ask Fredeema her business, she so trembled with fear that she could not utter a word. Then the old man, who had a kindly heart, spoke to her tenderly, and invited her into his cabin, where he told her she might have a home as long as she chose to stay, for he saw that she was in distress. After she had warmed herself by the fire, he prepared a frugal meal, the best his house afforded. Having now gained confidence, Fredeema told him who she was, and why she had come, and of all her wanderings in the wild and dismal forests with the fugitive Kushans. While they were talking, the old man's four sons, who lived with him, came in from their work, and listened to her story. They were enchanted with the fine, silver tones of her voice, and the way in which she pleaded the cause of the poor, despised Kushans drew forth all their sympathies. They admired the purity and uprightness of her sentiments, and her lofty and self-sacrificing benevolence. Old Ossamie perceived that they were deeply drinking in her spirit, but he sat quietly, and said not a word. As the evening wore away, he rose from his chair and took down a new hunting-rifle that hung in the room. Fredeema noticed a strange fire in his eye, and his determined look almost frightened her, though she knew, from his appearance, that he was meditating no harm to her. After burnishing his rifle, and putting his cartridges in order, he told Fredeema, that since her father had failed to act the part of a protector, as he was bound to do, and had sent her out into the cold world, he would himself adopt her as his own child, and would assume the right and the responsibility of a parent, to defend her against all that would do her harm. The brothers warmly responded, and assured her that she should ever be treated by them as a dear sister.

And now, my sons, said the old man, you had better get your weapons in readiness for fighting. This world is full of talk and sympathy, but talk and sympathy never yet protected the helpless. If you intend to deliver this hunted lamb from her persecutors, you must be prepared to do it at the risk of your lives. Blood is the purifier ordained to cleanse the stains of this bad world. See you not that the land is full of leprosy? It will require something more than water to wash it out. I am an old man, and my life is not worth much. You, my sons, are young; do as you like; but as for me, I shall set myself against the foul monster that is working all this mischief. I will make my way into his fortress; I will enter his palace; I will stand at his bedside; God helping me, I will send a shaft that shall wing its way to his heart; I will open the doors of his dungeons and knock off the fetters of his prisoners. And the boys said they would go with him. Then Ossamie reached up his hand and took down from the shelf a Book, which told of the Black Dragon, and of the Red Dragon, his father, and how they warred against the Lord, and how the judgments of Heaven should come down upon them in future times. After reading awhile, he fell upon his knees, as his custom was, and prayed the great Allfather that he would protect Fredeema, and deliver the Kushans for her sake, and that he would break the power of the Black Dragon, and banish him from Norland and from Sunland, and from all the green spots of creation, and seal him up in Tophet fast and forever.

When Fredeema saw into whose hands she had fallen, and what a high and noble nature the stern old man possessed, and felt her hopes of happiness and security once more revive, her heart throbbed wildly, for the joy was too great for her, and she burst into a flood of tears. Do not be excited, said Ossamie; compose yourself, trust in God and all will be well. So she dried up her tears, and when they had all bidden her a kind good-night she retired to rest. She soon fell into a sweet slumber, and dreamed of happy scenes in a world where all the inhabitants loved each other as brothers.

Ossamie immediately began to make preparations for invading the dominions of the Black Dragon. Inspired with his new idea, he visited all his old friends, and endeavored to rouse them to a common effort for the destruction of the monster. Many of them thought his aim was a good one, but disapproved of the means. In the first place, they thought it presumptuous for a few individuals to get up a crusade against such a venerable antediluvian, who was equal, and perhaps more than equal, in power and prestige to the sovereign himself. Secondly, if any thing was to be done, it should be done by the king of the country; and as he was at peace and amity with the Dragon, it would be treasonous for any of the common people to run counter to his example, or attempt to execute justice without his order. It was generally admitted that abstractly the Dragon had no right to oppress and maltreat the Kushaus; but as long as he did not meddle with the Normen and Norwomen, it was deemed highly impolitic to stir up his wrath by interfering in behalf of the wretched and helpless creatures who had the misfortune to fall under his power. So they told Ossamie plainly that they would have nothing to do with his schemes; most of them, indeed, thought that he was crazy, or would soon become so. A few people, who saw what a warm and generous heart he had, and how willing he was to sacrifice himself to help them that had no helper, encouraged him in his undertaking, and gave him money to buy weapons, long-shooters and short-shooters, and sharp lances with which the Kushans might defend themselves against their oppressors.

Meantime, the great princes and lords of the Dragonians, hearing that Fredeema had taken refuge with a woodsman of the west, sent forth their emissaries in great numbers, to search her out and bring her to the palace in chains, for the Dragon had now given up all idea of making her his wife, and was only bent upon destroying her and her friends. His bandits were ordered to plunder and lay waste the new country, and kill off the Fredonians as fast as they could. Great numbers were shot and gibbeted, storehouses emptied, and villages burnt, throwing the whole country into consternation. The sons of Ossamie were taken prisoners, their arms pinioned behind them with thongs that cut to the bone, and in this condition they were fastened to the Dragonians' horses, and made to run with them as they galloped away in the burning heat toward Sunland. One of them became a maniac from the heating of his brain; another was killed by a White devil-preacher, who thought it great merit to offer him as a sacrifice to his god.

At length Ossamie, having completed his arrangements, and fired anew by the barbarian cruelties inflicted on his sons and neighbors, arose suddenly and took his departure for Sunland, accompanied by three of his sons and his son-in-law, and a dozen trusty warriors. They came upon the Dragon's stronghold by night, gaining admission without difficulty. Carefully feeling their way, they entered an apartment near the palace, which was full of fire-arms and great guns and powder, first making prisoners of the watchmen who stood guard at the door. From this room they hoped to find a passage into the Dragon's bed-chamber, in which case they would soon be able to finish him. But in this expectation they were disappointed, and when the morning began to dawn they found their entrance had been discovered. The news flew like lightning through the palace and throughout all Sunland, and riders were hurrying to and fro, all wild as with the excitement of battle. When the Black Dragon heard the tumult and was told the cause, he roared with fury and lashed his tail against the palace-walls till they shook as if there had been an earthquake. The thunder of his roaring echoed even to the distant hills of Norland, causing the inhabitants to quake with terror and hide themselves within their houses. The Dragon also came forth of his palace and showed himself in all his gigantic proportions, his form towering aloft to the region of the stars, darkening the sun as a cloud, and throwing a gloomy shadow over the whole land. Poor Fredeema sat crouching, solitary and trembling, in a mountain cave ; none daring to minister to her wants, or inquire after her welfare, or even pronounce her name.

And now the governors and the generals and captains of Sunland, with an army of horsemen and footmen, began to gather from all quarters ; and they environed Ossamie and his companions, who fought bravely for their lives, but were at last overpowered. The sons of the old hero were slain, and he himself was captured, wounded and bleeding, and dragged to the council-house for examination. And the governor said to him, I know all about your villainy ; I want no information on that point ; but tell me, knave, who sent you hither ? You have come at the instigation of Samuncle ; it is of no use to deny it. Confess, and I will give you a fair trial. Then Ossamie, groaning with pain, turned his gory head and meekly replied, My deed is my own ; I have had no counsel or advice from Samuncle. Unless you will judge me according to justice, I wish no trial ; if you are determined to have my blood, kill me at once, for I am ready to die. The good Book tells me I should do to others as I would have others do to me; and in seeking to pluck the captives from the teeth of the Dragon, I have done no more than I should wish some kind deliverer to do for me in similar circumstances.

Then the governor, who was a Wiseman, said within himself, I must not seem to condemn this man for hating the Dragon and befriending the Kushans, lest it should create for him sympathizers even among ourselves; but I will try him for killing and murdering the soldiers that were sent against him. So he held a court, and brought lawyers and witnesses, and made a great parade of justice and legality, and finally adjudged him to death. Then they told him he must have the soul-doctors to convert and cleanse him, so that when he died he might not fall into the everlasting flames. But Ossamie would not hearken to their advice, and he returned for answer that he would give more for the prayer of a poor Kushan mother than for all the prayers and catechisms of all the soul-doctors the Black Dragon had in his employ.

At length the martyr was led forth to die, while a great army of soldiers and horsemen were paraded around him to witness the spectacle and triumph over his fate. And they hung him up between the heavens and the earth, and watched him until he was dead. But no sooner had the spirit escaped from the body than it spread abroad in the atmosphere, filling the winds with strange whispers, and flitting here and there, like a ghost, through all the land. It disturbed the lords and princes of the Dragon's court in their midnight dreams; and the young men and women of Norland began to breathe a fresher and purer air, and to feel new impulses, and to yearn after the long-loved and banished Fredeema. Within two years from Ossamie's death, the people had generally come to the conviction that he was yet hovering over the country in the shape of a guardian angel; that instead of retiring defeated from the contest with the Black Dragon, he had joined the army of the Lord; that his knapsack was still strapped upon his back, and his soul marching on.

CHAPTER V.

CORONATION OF MAGNUS MAHARBA.

AVING now become fully convinced that the affections of the Normen were inseparably twined around the gentle Fredeema, the Dragonians began to consult how they might break up the kingdom, and form a new government of which the Black Dragon should have the sole possession. Old Public Functionary, who had long been king of the United Occident, and who had offered two hundred and fifty silverlings for the capture of Ossamie, was about to end his reign, and there were gloomy apprehensions that his successor would not be so friendly to the Black Dragon as he had been. When the time came for appointing a new ruler, there was great excitement through the land. And on a set day the various tribes assembled, the Dragonians, and the Democrians, and the Fredonians, and the Publicans, and the Eradicators, and the Conservators, and the multitudes of the people both in Norland and Sunland, to witness the casting of the lots. And many of them sat up watching all night, while the seers and augurs consulted the omens. And when the morning was come, behold the air was full of falling leaves, which the wind had blown far and wide over the country. And when the people had picked them up, and examined them carefully, they found writ-

ten upon them the name of MAGNUS MAHARBA. So they knew that this was the name of their next king.

Then was there great commotion in the palace of the Dragon, and the lords and princes and ladies of his household were filled with indignation, for they had heard of Magnus Maharba, that he was an honest man, and one that loved justice and equity, and hence they inferred that he must be an enemy of their master. They had also heard it reported that Fredeema, during her travels, had spent a night at his house, and instilled into his mind her fanatical plans for letting loose the Kushans, and leaving the Dragon to die of starvation. So the chiefs and nobles assembled and drew up the charter of a new kingdom for the support and defense of their august patron and his progeny, and for the extension of his and their glory, influence and power over all the lands and seas, and for the extermination of their enemies by fire and sword. And they chose Prince Jeffer to be their king, and his chief ministers were Lord Sepulchre, and Lord Judas, and Moneymonger, and Navymalady, whose office it was to make desolate the seas and to bury in deep waters the ships of Samuncle. And for his generals he had Greatbrag, and Prettyguard, and Stonyjohn, and Stonyjack, and Boldrobin. And they raised a great army and took possession of the strongholds and castles, and seized many ships and guns, besides those which had been secretly given them by the servants of Public Functionary.

Now when the lords and councilors of the Occidentals, who were assembled in parliament, heard these things, they were filled with alarm. And they said among themselves, we must by all means pacify the Dragon, and give him whatever he demands; otherwise we shall have war and bloodshed, and our happy land will become a land of strife and tumult, like the ancient kingdoms of the Orient. After much angry debate, some being in favor of the Dragon and some against him, they agreed to make a treaty of perpetual peace and amity on these conditions, namely, that his majesty the Dragon was to be recognized as sovereign of the country conjointly with the reigning king; but he was not to stretch his arms or feet, or the shadow of his authority, over any of the new western lands that had been purchased by Samuncle; secondly, that Fredeema should be given him to wife, according to the original agreement; lastly, that the Normen should enter into a solemn covenant with the Dragon that they would not molest him in the future, nor speak of him disrespectfully as they had done; and would under no circumstances allow any flying Kushans to take refuge in their borders; and that this covenant should never be altered, while sun, moon and stars shone in the heavens, or while mountains, seas and rivers marked the divisions of the earth. So they sent out the decree north, south, east, and west, that all the land might confirm it.

But it was now too late; for the Black Dragon, seeing the cowardice and consternation of the king and his council, began to stretch himself more and more, and declared that he would accept of nothing less than undivided sway from ocean to ocean, straight across the continent, and from where the northern lion shakes his snowy mane to where the southern alligator suns himself on the sandy shore of the Great Basin. The Normen also were displeased with the new covenant, and refused to confirm it. And the powerful Samuncle began to show his spirit, and to deny that he had ever promised his daughter in marriage to the Dragon; for his heart smote him when he heard of the cruel sufferings to which Fredeema had been exposed in her wanderings, and he reproached himself for the cowardly part he had acted in sending her off, instead of manfully standing up and protecting her with the brawny muscles of his strong arm. At last he went to the attorneys and to the ancients that were skilled in the law, and desired them to examine the parchments of betrothal by which it was claimed that his daughter had been consigned in wedlock to the snaky monster. After diligent search and careful deciphering of the manuscripts, the lawyers gave their opinion that no evidence of a betrothal existed, and that the documents relied on to prove it had no valid bearing on the case. Then said Samuncle, " God forgive me that I have acted like a fool; Fredeema shall return, and I will defend her, if need be, with my life."

When the time came for Magnus Maharba to ascend the throne, all the omens were unpropitious. The sky lowered, the clouds shot forth lightnings, thunder, muttered, vipers and rattlesnakes came hissing from their dens, and the high-priest, that was to pour on his head the anointing oil, was a Dark diabolical Dragonian. Now Magnus Maharba was of a 'quiet and peaceful temper, he loved every body, and sought the good of all men, and his greatest care was that he might never injure an enemy, but with even-handed justice treat friend and foe alike. No king had ever before held the scales of justice with so impartial a hand. In his heart he hated the Black Dragon; but inasmuch as he had been constituted king over both good and bad, he was resolved that bad and good should equally share his protection. He had learned from the priests and soul-doctors that when the Almighty fashioned their planet with his fingers, and rolled it out from the depths of ether, a molten and fiery ball, even then he ordained it to be the future habitation of the Black Dragon, and predestined that kings and princes should do him honor, and should protect him, and should allow him a certain portion of their race for his workmen, and for his wood and water carriers, and for his maid-servants, and for merchandise, and for sacrifice on his altars, and for whatever purposes he might find it convenient to use them. But the Eradicators told the king that the soul-doctors were wrong; that the Dragon; was a usurper and an outlaw; that he was not a creature of God but of the devil; and that it would be right to kill him and throw out his carcass to bleach in the rains of heaven with the carcasses of the poor innocents whom he had murdered. The king lent a willing ear to these opinions, for he abhorred oppression; and although he thought it would be wrong for him to take the life of one of God's creatures over whom he had been placed as a ruler, yet he secretly wished that God himself, if he disapproved of the Dragon's doings, would send down a thunderbolt to destroy him, and thus relieve the land of its foulest and worst enemy.

When Magnus Maharba was anointed king, he stood up on the throne, and made a speech to the people, according to the custom of the country, so that all might understand the principles of his government and what was to be the manner of his rule. He told them that he would not allow Norland and Sunland to be divided, for he had taken his oath to preserve them in union as one country; yet he would grant the Dragonians every indulgence that was possible. Although the Black Dragon was offensive to the Normen, his rights should be respected; and if any of his captives escaped, they should be hunted up and restored to him; and the people of Sunland should be left to manage their own affairs as they saw fit, provided they would not seize the forts and castles belonging to the king, nor interfere with the ships and trading of Samuncle.

Thus kindly did the new king endeavor to allay the irritation of the Dragonians, but to no purpose. They answered him back with scorn that he was no king of theirs; that they had not chosen, nor would they accept him; that they had provided a government for themselves; and as for the king's power to enforce a union between them and the Normen, they defied him. And they gathered their fleets and armies, and set them in battle array against the king's garrison, for they were impatient to begin the war.

CHAPTER VI.

COMMENCEMENT OF THE DRAGONIAN WAR.

N the eastern coast of Sunland stood Stonepile Castle, one of the king's strongholds, built by Samuncle at great expense, as a safeguard against foreign invaders. It rose from the waters at the mouth of a river, and was guarded by the servants of Samuncle, who had orders to admit no visitors, nor allow any vessels to pass without the king's permission. And the Dragon sent a messenger to the captain of the garrison, saying, " Give me the key of the castle, that my warriors may enter in and occupy it, for it is built upon my territory, and therefore belongs to me." And the captain, and they that were with him, refused, for they said, " We must obey the orders of our king, and without his permission we can give admittance to no one." And Prince Jeffer said, " Now is our time; let us storm the castle, and so bring on war, and then will all the people of Sunland be united as one man, and we will fire their hearts against the tyrant Maharba, and will go out against him in battle, and will overthrow and destroy him, and will enter his palace and rule the whole land." And he gave the command, and Duke Prettyguard surrounded the castle, and bombarded it with his artillery, and threw upon it shells and combustibles, setting it on fire, and filling it with smoke

and flames. And he drove out the men that were set to guard it, and tore down the king's banner, and put in its place the banner of the Rattlesnake and Dragon. And they shouted and sang, and made merry over their victory.

And when Magnus Maharba saw what was done, he sent word to Samuncle, and bade him go through the land and collect threescore and fifteen thousand warriors to fight for their king and country, and to recover the forts and castles that had been captured. Then was Samuncle glad, for he had long been impatient to avenge the insults of the Dragonians, and had been angry with the king for his extreme forbearance. He had also told his friends privately that Father Magnus should not restrain him much longer, for if he could not obtain redress otherwise, he would take the law into his own hands. As soon as he received the king's mandate to summon the warriors, he rose up in haste to execute the commission. And there was tramping to and fro, and messengers hurrying over plain and mountain, and the air was alive with the sound of mustering footsteps, and the rattling and burnishing of weapons.

And Samuncle consulted with the rich men of Gotham, and he counseled them to open the cellars where they kept their treasures, and bring out the gold that was hid behind their Walls, and give it into the hand of the king's officers for purchasing weapons, and for building ships, and for clothing and feeding the warriors. And they answered him favorably, and promised to give the king all that he needed.

Now the city of Gotham was a Babelitish city, and the language of the people discordant. And many of them were Dragonians, who appeared in the garb of Democrians, resembling them so closely that the common people could scarcely tell the difference. The merchants and mariners were generally friends of the

Dragon, because their wealth was made by trafficking in the scales which fell from his body, for he shed his scales every year, and they were of a fine and beautiful texture, and susceptible of a great variety of color and polish, and when manufactured into robes and vestments were much admired and sought after by the merchants of foreign countries. The Dragon had now put a stop to this traffic; many, therefore, who had previously advocated his cause, suddenly turned against him, declaring that they had always disliked him in their hearts, and that henceforth they abjured and renounced him forever. They even went so far as to say that it was not fit that such a monster should live. The three wise men of Gotham, at whose lips the people were accustomed to take advice, and whose names were Timeservitor, Tribunosopher, and Harlequin, had until now been divided in counsel. One recommended gentleness and forbearance toward the Dragon; another was willing the monster and all that loved him should depart and be gone, and form a pandemonium for themselves, such as they chose; while the third refused to give advice either way, not knowing whether King Magnus or Prince Jeffer would prove the stronger. But when they saw the king's flag torn down, and the soldiers of Samuncle fired upon and driven out of their castle, and the rattlesnakes triumphing over its ruins, these three. wise men stood up with united voice, and bade the people come forward at the call of their king, and wash out the stain on their banner with the blood of those that had insulted it. And the multitude rushed with one impulse into the councilgrove, and the chief warriors, and the old men, and the merchants, and the lawyers and spiritual doctors harangued them there, and exhorted them to fight for their altars and inheritances, and the covenant of their fathers. And the grove resounded with shouts, and tri colored banners were hung upon every tree, and the people lifted up their hands toward heaven, and took a solemn oath that they would allow no Dragon kingdom to be established upon their soil. And the governor of the city, whose name was Rottenwood, a chief of the Dragonians, was there; and when the multitude discovered him they crowded around him and threatened him, and told him that he also should raise his voice for his king and country, or else be counted for a traitor. So they compelled him to mount the vinegar barrel and shout for Magnus Maharba and Samuncle.

And the great army of Samuncle was gathered according to the king's commandment, and they commenced their march into Sunland. But the generals were cautioned to deal gently with the lords and princes of the Dragonians, and on no account to make war upon the Dragon himself, but only to show him how impotent he was to contend with the forces of the king, and thus frighten him into good behavior, if he could not be won by kindness. And when Duke Bottleholder and Duke Micklemackle entered into the Dragonian country, they first of all issued their proclamations, enjoining upon their followers and all the people to honor and respect the authority of the Black Dragon, and warning the Kushans that if they improved the opportunity of their master's distress to rise against him, they would be crushed with an iron hand. But while the chiefs of the Normen were so tender of the Dragon, and so careful to injure his lords and noblemen as little as possible, the Dragonians fought with their utmost strength and fury, showing favor neither to high nor low.

When the king saw that all the small battles were going against him, and that instead of being impressed with a wholesome dread of his power, the Dragonians were only the more emboldened, he called for Duke Doitwell, and bade him commence the war in earnest. And he sent him with two score and ten legions of stalwart warriors, ordering him to make an overwhelming assault on the central Dragonian army, and after defeating, to pursue them even to the gates of Richmantown, their capital. Then Duke Doitwell crossed over the Boundarymark river and entered Virginland. After marching two days he came to a small stream called Bullscamper, on the other side of which lay the Dragonians strongly fortified, and ready for an attack. And the Normen advanced and fought them three days and three nights, but could not dislodge them, for their chiefs were old warriors, thoroughly skilled in their art, and they warily kept to their intrenchments, and would not fight on the open field. But on the fourth day they marched out and joined battle, and fought with desperation; and there was a great slaughter. And when the sun was going down, and the Normen were faint and weary, they saw a spectre named Pan, and trembled with great fear. And when a few of them began to fly, the terror spread among the rest, and they looked this way and that, and lo! the spectre was close upon them. And they gave a cry, and threw away their guns and knapsacks, and abandoned their wagons and cannon, and ran as if the earth were cleaving asunder behind them; they paused neither to eat or drink till they got back to the royal city. But their enemies did not pursue them, for they thought it was a ruse. And the next morning they sent forth their scouts to examine the battle-field, and to find where the Normen were. And when they had fully searched the region around, and saw that the army of Samuncle had indeed gone back, leaving the roadside strewn with garments and weapons hurriedly cast away, their courage revived, and they shouted and danced, and proclaimed a great victory, and all Sunland was filled with songs and festivity.

And they gathered their slain and wounded and

buried the dead. But many of the Normen were left above ground, and when the flesh had decayed and fallen off, they carried the bones to their tents, and manufactured them into drinking-cups, and finger-rings, and necklaces, and all manner of curious ornaments to present to their wives and sweethearts, as tokens of their valor, and to hang up as trophies in their colleges and museums, along with the skin of Ossamie's son, and the scalps and skeletons of others that had been sacrificed in honor of their god.

CHAPTER VII.

BLOODY BATTLES IN VIRGINLAND.

ORTIFIED and confounded at the unlooked-for disaster of Bullscamper, the king and his lords and his parliament began to doubt whether they should be able to frighten the Dragon out of his insolence by killing off a portion of his servants and adherents, and whether it would not be better to make war directly upon the monster himself. But the king said, Let us do justly, and let us spare his life if possible. I have taken an oath to preserve him, according to the ancient statutes; yet notwithstanding this, my obligation to the country is greater than to him. It is the physician's duty to save his patient with his limbs entire if he can; but if he finds this impossible, then he is justified in cutting off the limb to save the man's life. So will I do with the Dragon; when it becomes certain that I cannot save him without endangering the kingdom, I will leave him to his fate, and his violence shall come down upon his own head, and I shall be guiltless of his blood. Then said the king's counselors, Let a part of the Dragon's power be taken away, and let some of his lands be confiscated, and let as many of the Kushans as are forced to help him in his wicked war be released from their bondage, and be invited to take shelter under the starry banner,

and forever after let them be free from the service and authority of their cruel masters. Thus shall we touch the Dragon in a tender spot, and he will become alarmed, and will be compelled to sue for peace on such terms as we may dictate. And the king gave his consent, and they wrote the decree, and it was recorded among the statutes of the realm.

Soon after this one of the king's chieftains, whose name was Duke Freemantle, being on a march in the west, discovered one of the Dragon's long arms extended out into the new country, and grasping a stake which he had planted there as a sign of his lawful possession. And Duke Freemantle called for his staff, and hasted and ran, and laid hold on the gigantic paw, and bound it fast to the stake, and gave orders to his officers that they should bring swords and axes and knives, and cut it off. Then the Dragon howled with a bitter and most lamentable howl, that reached even to the palace, and fell upon the ears of the king. And when the king had inquired and learned the cause, he sent a messenger to Duke Freemantle, and rebuked him, and ordered him to release the Dragon's limb, and in nowise to sever it from his body, as the wound might prove fatal, and then he would be guilty of the Dragon's blood. But Freemantle would not loose the bands, for he regarded the slaying of such a monster as no murder. Nevertheless, out of respect to the king's orders, he allowed the paw to remain as it was, until Duke Huntsman was sent to unbind the ropes and give the old reprobate another chance for his life.

But all the king's kindness had no effect upon the Dragon, for he was as proud and imperious as ever. Then the king called for five hundred legions of warriors, in addition to those he already had, and he took two hundred legions of the bravest, and placed Duke Micklemackle at their head, and ordered them to march valiantly but warily, and take possession of the enemy's capital. And Duke Micklemackle said to the king, I must train and teach them before I can lead them to meet the Dragonians, lest they should not be able to withstand the sharp edge of battle, and should be thrown into confusion as at Bullscamper, and we be again brought to shame.

And the money in the king's coffers began to grow scant, and the gold ceased to flow from behind the Walls of Gotham, and from the vaults of Brothercity and Bosstown and Shipcargo, and the river banks, where the king's officers had digged so successfully, yielded no more. Then Magnus Maharba made his wants known to his ministers and wise men, and they said, Was not money in ancient time obtained from the mouth of a fish? And to whom should the king look for silver and gold but to Lord Greenfish, whom he has appointed to be over his treasury? And the great council passed a decree that the lord treasurer should be required to replenish the exhausted chests, and that he should be permitted to manufacture money out of whatever materials he found most convenient, and that any substance stamped and coined in the treasury mills should be counted for the true coin and currency of the realm. And Lord Greenfish multiplied his mills, and cast therein old clothes and divers linen and cotton fabrics, and there came out beautiful soft money, stamped with images of the king and his lords, and illustrated with all manner of strange and curious devices. And the color of it was green, like the color of the ocean. And when the king saw it he was well satisfied, and Samuncle took it and circulated it through the country, and the people were delighted; and they used it for traffic, and for the payment of tribute and customs, and no longer complained of their burdens.

Lord Seawarder was also one of the chief ministers

of the realm, and he was appointed to watch the kings and countries beyond the seas, and to prevent their sending over vessels and rendering assistance to the Dragon. And Lord Deepwater had charge of the ships of Samuncle, and he sent them to guard the eastern coast of Sunland, and to throw fiery missiles upon the Dragonians, and to drive them out of their cities, and to retake the fortresses of Samuncle which had been stolen from him. And the vessels scoured along the shore, and went around to the south of Sunland; and entering into the Great Basin they passed on and came to the mouth of Fatherwater river, on the bank of which lay the great city of Feveropolis. And Duke Bottleholder went up with the ships, and stormed the fortresses and took the city, and held it in the name of King Magnus Maharba. And he ruled the enemies of the king with rigor, both Hesesh and Shesesh; but he governed the people righteously, and delivered the Kushans out of the hands of their oppressors.

While the ships were thus making conquests on the southern shore, Duke Micklemackle remained in the royal city, carefully training his two hundred legions, so that when the spring opened he might move them forward to Richmantown. As soon as the winter had passed, the king ordered him to make haste and be gone, and told him that since he was afraid to lead his warriors by the way of Bullscamper, where they had seen the spectre, he might take them around by ship to the east of the enemy's city, and march from thence by a short and easy road. So they took ship and landed on the eastern shore of Virginland, and marched toward the Dragon's stronghold. And when Duke Micklemackle had come near to the city, and beheld the spires of the temples, and the fortifications behind which the Dragon had intrenched himself, and the vast armies that were gathered around the place for its defense, and could discern the forms of the horses and horsemen that were moving in the distance, and the open mouths of the great black guns, his heart sunk within him, and the joints of his knees became loose and his limbs tottering. And he called for a spade, and said to his warriors, What you see me do, that do ye also. And he began to dig in the earth, and to cast up a bank before him; and when he had attained a sufficient depth, he sat down in the excavation, and was securely protected against any missiles which the enemy could hurl at him. And they all did so; and his warriors dug for themselves comfortable holes in which they might crouch and be secure. And they were well pleased for a time; but the soil was swampy, and their hiding-places became damp and unwholesome, and they were attacked with fevers and rheumatisms, and began to perish by hundreds in a day. And whenever a warrior died they covered him up in his hole, and leveled the earth above him, as it was before the digging. And upon a clear morning Duke Micklemackle arose early and looked over the plain, and lo, the ground was all becoming smooth and level, and in some places scarce a single open hole was to be seen. Then he perceived that if he remained a few weeks longer, the meadows would be restored to their original beauty and stillness, and be greener and grassier than ever, and he would have accomplished nothing except the burial of his warriors beneath them. And when he thought on the answer he should make to the king, and how he could account for the loss of his army, he was filled with the most gloomy anticipations.

And now the enemy's horsemen began to crowd around him more closely, galloping in his rear every night, and threatening to cut off his retreat. Then he saw plainly that he must either fight or fly. At last he remembered having heard of a fine river which lay about four days' journey to the south, and after consulting his chief captains, he determined to march across the swamps and morasses to find it. So he put his warriors in motion, and they plunged boldly into the bogs and fens, where they soon became enveloped in cloud and mist, and in dense forests covered with hanging moss which the sun could scarcely penetrate. They also heard terrible howlings by night, and spectres and goblins were perpetually flitting across their paths, and those that were sick and feeble were tormented with the horrible apprehension that they should be left behind to become a prey for the wild beasts and monsters of the wood.

As soon as the Dragonians saw that the Normen had entered the swamps they clapped their hands for joy, and rushed after them, and overtook them, and attacked them before and behind, and planted their cannon against them, and fought them day after day, and chased them with their cavalry, and cut down and butchered great numbers. But the troops of Samuncle stood their ground bravely, and hurled back their pursuers once and again with fearful slaughter. And desperation gave firmness to their hearts, and changed their sinews to steel, and they grew so accustomed to fight that they flinched not from combat with man, goblin, or demon, and would have fought the Red Dragon of Tophet himself, if he had come in their path. And they wrote their victories on the Pines and the Oaks, and swept through the forest with a thundering tramp as of conquerors in the hour of their glory. But they left behind them many of their best and bravest, who laid themselves down to die in miry fens, or were mingled with their foes among the heaps of slain.

And on the seventh day they emerged from the swamps and forests, and behold, the banks of the beautiful river were before them. And Duke Micklemackle, being on horseback, rode on before the rest, and reaching the river first, he found there a war-boat of Samuncle, into which he entered and was safe. And other ships and boats were procured, and the remnant of the great army entered into them and returned to the royal city. And Duke Micklemackle presented them before the king, and told him of the courage and gallantry they had displayed, and of the victories they had won. But when Magnus Maharba looked upon them, and saw how their ranks were thinned, he was much displeased, and he wept for grief and shame that his warriors had been sacrificed, and yet the object for which he sent them had not been accomplished.

CHAPTER VIII.

SAMUNCLE PLEADS FOR FREDEEMA.

HEN Samuncle heard of this fresh disaster, and saw the shattered legions returning from Virginland, his indignation was aroused, and he hastened to the palace while his heart was yet hot; and when he had forced his way into the king's presence, he addressed him and said, O King Magnus Maharba, were you not anointed ruler and chief over this people for their protection and for their good? And how is it that you are making these holocausts to an infernal Dragon, giving up your subjects to be sacrificed by thousands and tens of thousands, even a hundred thousand in a year, rather than allow us to kill the vile creature that has instigated this cruel war, and is now seeking to take the king's life, as well as the lives of his people? And how is it that you have sent Duke Micklemackle, the enemy of the Kushans, and an old and intimate acquaintance of the Dragon, to bury the soldiers I have given you in swamps and marshes and ignoble graves? And why is not the trumpet blown for the Kushans, to summon them into the ranks of the warriors, to fight for their king and his kingdom? Are they not strong and courageous? Are they not true and faithful, and have they not many times released the feet of the king's servants from the gins and

traps of their enemies? And why should the Dragon be allowed to grind their faces, and break their bones and devour them? Are they not flesh and blood like ourselves? Have they not human feelings? Do they not laugh when they are merry, and weep when they are sad? Do they not suffer when they are starved? Do not their backs smart when the whip tears their skin? Do their bodies burn without pain? How is it that a king who loves justice and equity has no pity for the sorrows of these innocents? Had the king but proclaimed the Dragon a monster and an outlaw when he first began the war, and called out the Kushans to avenge themselves of their oppressors, our troubles would have long since ended; the monster would have been slain, and the widows and orphans, whose husbands and fathers I persuaded to enter this conflict, would not now be filling my ears with their wailings and reproaches. Why should the king continue to show kindness to the Black Dragon? Do you still purpose to give my daughter Fredeema to his unnatural embrace? Will you seek for other records of betrothal, since it is found that the old covenant gives the ·Dragon no claim?

Then Magnus Maharba, who saw that Samuncle was greatly excited, answered him meekly and said, Remember, good friend, that you yourself have acknowledged your promise to give your daughter in marriage to the Black Dragon; you have repeatedly averred that this was your understanding of the covenant; you have sent out your servants to hunt up the fugitives and return them to bondage; you have cheerfully paid taxes and tribute for supporting the Dragon, and have shared in his profits; and now will you disavow your own words and repudiate your obligations?

Then Samuncle colored deeply, for his conscience condemned him, and he could not answer a word.

The king continued: You say it is wrong to oppress

the Kushans, and to extort from them labor without wages. This is what I have always thought; but the soul-doctors tell me it is right, and that the Dragon was made by the Creator for this very purpose, and that the sacred books confirm it beyond question. And when I myself see that God has allowed the Dragon to exist for so many ages, and still keeps him in being, I am led to doubt whether he hates the creature as much as I do; for if it had been left to me, I would have put him out of the way long ago. But I have no power over the Dragon, and what would it avail if I should say to the Kushans, You are now delivered, your dungeon is unlocked, your chains are broken? Would my saying so make it so? Should I not be like the famous Bullfighter who attached his animal to a paper kite and sent it up to stop the comet? I cannot even send a messenger to Richmantown; my soldiers have been trying for a year, and cannot get there. How am I to reach the Kushans and tell them they are released from the authority of their oppressors?

But Samuncle was not satisfied, and he said they might as well stop fighting, if they were still determined to remain in friendship with the Dragon and reject the friendship of the Kushans. And he went away downcast and heavy hearted, displeased with the king for his conscientiousness, and cursing the day that he had ever been duped by bad advisers to enter into partnership with Old Scaly.

When Samuncle was gone the king began to reflect bitterly on the condition of his country, and the miseries the Black Dragon had brought upon it, and he inquired within himself, Is it right that all my subjects should perish for the sake of one, and that one the most hateful of all, a tyrant and an enemy, whose destruction would, beyond dispute, be a public benefit? Am I not doing wrong to Samuncle and Fredeema, and to the people of the land, by sacrificing them at the shrine of this bloody Moloch? Does not my oath to protect all the inhabitants require that I should punish those who injure the rest? If the Dragon is entitled to my protection, is he not also liable to penalties for his robberies and his murders and his rebellions?

And the king could not sleep that night, for the multitude of thoughts that pressed on his memory, and for pity of the wretched Fredeema, whose cries for protection he had so long disregarded; and he now began to reproach himself for having coldly turned her away, when he should have cherished her as his best friend. After revolving the matter in his brain for a long time, he finally concluded that he would indulge the Black Dragon in his waywardness no longer; that he would appoint him a day for repentance and reconciliation, and after that if he should persist in his wicked and wanton war, he would issue a decree for his expulsion from the fair plains of Sunland, where he had set up his authority, and for the liberation of all the Kushans that were pining in bondage.

And when the morning was come the king arose early, and entered into his closet, and put his thoughts to writing in the form of a proclamation, offering a free pardon to the Dragon and his adherents, and setting him a time to desist from his warfare and become reconciled to Samuncle, and warning him of his fate if he should still longer refuse. And he called his lords together for counsel, and showed them what he had written. And none of them said aught against it, for they saw that the king's resolution was fixed. They were also glad that the Dragon was at last to meet his deserts. Then said Lord Seawarder, for he was wise and far-seeing, and understood times and seasons, The offer and warning which the king purposes to make to the Black Dragon are good, but the time is not propitious. For the armies of the king are now driven back, and the Dragonian captains and horsemen are pressing upon us sorely, even to the gates of the capital, and the hearts of the people are melted like wax. And when the news of this threatening is spread abroad, all men will say it is the king's last cry of despair, for he is subdued by the Dragonians, and in his extremity he looks to the Kushans for help; not that he cares for the Kushans, or desires to protect them, neither has he any respect or pity for the wandering and wretched Fredeema, but selfishness and fear constrain him. So the nations will scorn us, and the people of Sunland will triumph over us and mock our impotency, and grow bolder in fight than before. Rather let the king wait for a more auspicious season; and let our generals roll back the tide of war into the enemy's country, and let our invincible hosts again stand before Richmantown. When this advantage is gained, let the king issue his proclamation and his warning, and ordain liberty to the captives, and all the Kushans will rush to join us, and the Dragon race shall quake throughout all Sunland, and then as conquerors we will prescribe the conditions of peace. And the king said, This counsel is good; we will wait for the better time.

CHAPTER IX.

DRAGONIAN INVASION OF NORLAND.

RINCE JEFFER and the Dragon were now in close consultation; and when they saw the discomfiture of the Normen, and how they had gathered around their capital in terror, they laid their plans for invading and conquering all Norland. And they sent off Boldrobin in haste, and ordered him to lay waste the towns and cities, and seize the silver and gold, and the flocks and herds, and every thing upon which his warriors could lay their hands. And being exceedingly puffed up with vainglory, Prince Jeffer gave orders that they should take captive Magnus Maharba himself, and bring him in chains, that he might show him to the Dragon.

Meanwhile the king, perceiving the danger of leaving an open road by which his enemies might advance to attack the capital, had sent off another army towards Richmantown, by the way of Bullscamper, to drive back the haughty hosts that were rushing over the Rapidrun and Rapidknocking rivers, and through the valley of the Shiningdoor. And he divided the army into bands, and placed over them Dukes Pontiff and Doitwell and Strongbeer, and other brave generals. And the king said it was fitting that the Pontiff should be above the rest, so he gave him the chief command. But Duke

Pontiff was a young warrior, and the older chiefs were jealous, and displeased that a stripling should be placed over them.

And when he reached the Rapidknocking river, he assembled his legions and harangued them, and told them, as Duke Micklemackle had done before, that they had met their last defeat, and made their last retreat; that disasters were all in the rear, but glory in the front, and that the chaplets of victory would soon be wreathed around their brows. So he spread out his army along the river bank, to prevent the Dragonians from crossing; but they came on like locusts, and while he was guarding one spot they dashed over in another. And when he saw how greatly their numbers exceeded his own, he became alarmed, and sent and besought Duke Micklemackle to give him more warriors, and food for his men and horses. But Duke Micklemackle said he should have known better than to go that way, and now he might get himself back as he could.

Then Duke Pontiff saw that he was in an evil case, and he gathered his warriors around him, two score and ten legions, and fought the second great battle of Bullscamper against an overwhelming multitude of Dragonians. And Duke Strongbeer stood aloof and would not help him in his extremity; but Duke Doitwell, and Duke Henchman, and Horntosser, and Sharpsickle, and the other dukes and captains fought valiantly, and kept up the fight seven days. For they said, We must now retrieve the disasters that befell us last year by reason of the spectre. But when they beheld the cohorts of the Dragonians multiplying, and coming on by tens and hundreds of thousands, and saw the towering plumes of Boldrobin, and the majestic strides of Longstep, and heard the thundering of Stonyjack's cavalry, they perceived their case was hopeless. And gathering up the remnants of their broken bands, they made their way back, as best they could, and betook themselves for shelter to the strongholds on the banks of the Boundary-mark.

Following sharp after the king's army rushed the legions of Stonyjack and Longstep, with Boldrobin behind them. Through the Shiningdoor valley and over the Boundarymark river they swept like a whirlwind. And ten thousand of the Norland warriors were keeping guard in the valley of the Harpers, and they were harping and singing songs in praise of Samuncle and Fredeema, and of Ossamie the Martyr, for that was the spot where he fell. And the Dragonians surrounded them, and took them captive, and bade them hang their harps on the willows and sing no more.

And the king was sorely perplexed and sick at heart, and he went into his closet and shut the door, and prayed to the God of heaven, and vowed a vow, saying, If God will but give me relief this once, then will I no longer delay, but will appoint the Dragon his day, and after allowing him space for repentance, I will proclaim a decree of outlawry against him, and he shall be exterminated and destroyed, and hung up as a spectacle in the sight of all nations.

And the king was in a great strait, for he had no general on whom he could rely to lead his warriors at such a critical time. For Duke Micklemackle had returned in dishonor from Richmantown, and besides that, he was very tender of the Dragonians, and he had warned the king not to make war upon the Dragon's own royal person, but only to terrify him somewhat by driving back his armies. Nor was the king willing to intrust the command to Dukes Pontiff and Doitwell, who had already been tried and found unable to cope with the daring prowess of Boldrobin. So he called his counselors, Lord Seawarder, and Lord Blaringtrump, and Lord Stampon, that was the king's army-scribe. Then said Lord Stampon, We must have a new chief. But the others preferred Duke Micklemackle; for they said, He is a Democrian, and if we dismiss him all the Democrians will desert the king, and then will it be worse with us than it is now. And the king said, Right; it is not wise to swap horses in the middle of a stream. So Duke Micklemackle was sent forward with a great army, and he encountered the Dragonians in the Southern mountains of Middleland, and set in array against them Horntosser with his legions, and Frankman, and Burningbrand, and they made a great slaughter of the invaders, and chased them up the sides of the mountains, and over the rocky crests, and down into the valley behind them, where was a small river called Anteaters' Creek. Then Boldrobin crossed the stream, and took possession of the hills that lay in the form of a crescent on the western bank, and prepared for a great battle. And the king's army encamped on the eastern side, and laid themselves down to rest for the night, saying, Tomorrow is the day of war, which is Woden's.

And when the eye-opener began to climb over the eastern hills, the warriors roused from their slumbers and commenced the fight. And the battle waxed fearfully bloody, and continued all day. On the north, Horntosser raged like a maddened bull, and swept down the Dragonians with his artillery; but he was at length wounded, and many of his captains were slain. And when Duke Summoner saw it, he summoned his band of veterans, and pressed forward to fill up the vacant ranks and hold fast the ground that had been won.

Now when the noontide was past, the Dragonian columns rolled toward the south, and there they fell upon Burningbrand, who was crossing the river on a stone bridge, in order to cut off their retreat. Here they fought till the sun went down; and the king's troops rested on their arms, expecting to renew the battle on the morrow. But on the morrow no battle came, for Boldrobin had disappeared. Then said Burningbrand and Horntosser, Now is our time to be up and after them. But Duke Micklemackle said, No, we are not able; for the Dragonians are strong, and they will lead us into an ambush; so he let them depart in quiet. And they returned and went to their own country, and reported to Prince Jeffer and the Dragon the misfortunes that had befallen them.

When Magnus Maharba saw that his prayer was answered, and that God had given him the victory over his enemies, he remembered his vow that he had made, and he sent for his scribes and caused them to copy the writing he had written, that it might be scattered among the people. And he said within himself, Now will I divide my enemies, and I will offer a reward to those that shall forsake the Black Dragon and return unto me; and when I have by this means recovered a portion of them, I can easily subdue the remainder. So he caused the writing to be wisely and carefully worded, promising to the people of all the provinces that should renounce and abjure the supremacy of the Dragon, and in token of their obedience send up their messengers to the great council, that the past should be forgiven, and they should be allowed to make their own government, and to manage their own affairs as aforetime. And if they now submitted they should be permitted to retain their helots in service; or if they would consent to release them for a ransom, then he would procure from the great council the price at which they should be valued, and after that the captives should go free, and he would transport them to their ancient country, or to some other happy clime. But for the Dragon, and those who continued to fight his battles, and to kill the soldiers of Samuncle, after the period of one hundred days, which would terminate on the first day of the Gate month of the next new year, there should be no pardon, and all the helots that served them should be set free without a ransom, and should be at liberty to go where they pleased, and the king's armies should not restore them to their oppressors, but should protect and defend them in their freedom; and thus the power and glory of the Dragon would be brought to an end, and he would perish and become extinct, for his pride and for his treason, and for his crime which he had committed in rebelling against the authority and government of the king.

CHAPTER X.

PAINFUL SUSPENSE OF FREDEEMA.

AMUNCLE and his daughter were now summoned to the palace. And the king showed them the writing he had written; and he said to Samuncle, Fredeema shall no longer be a fugitive and a vagabond; henceforth she shall abide in my palace as a daughter. For the Black Dragon has killed and destroyed our people, and has rendered himself unworthy of protection; nevertheless, it would not be right to depose and banish him without giving him a fair opportunity for repentance and reconciliation. I have therefore given him a hundred days of grace; let all things remain as they were till the time be past, and then I will issue my decree, and depose him from his princely state. And for Fredeema's sake I will ransom the Kushans from their bondage; and I will purchase for them some happy island whither they may betake themselves and be no more oppressed, and the tender heart of your gentle daughter shall be no longer chafed and torn with the cries and sufferings of the innocent.

Then said Samuncle, The word of the king is good; but suppose the Dragon should accept your offer, and the provinces and people send up their messengers before the opening of the Gate month, shall every thing then be restored as before? Shall the lives of my soldiers have been sacrificed for nought? Shall the Kushans, who have befriended them, and loosed their feet from the snares, be again returned to bondage? Shall the ancient covenant be revived, and Fredeema be united for life to the hideous old monster? For know, O King, that the Black Dragon shall never receive the hand of my daughter in marriage; and more than that, after what has happened, he and she cannot live upon the same continent; and still further, as my name is Samuncle, and as the blood of a giant race flows through my veins, this arm shall hunt him from shore to shore, till his carcass is buried five thousand fathoms deep in the salt sea, along with the hundred thousand whitening skeletons of his miserable victims, not yet covered by the ensepulchering ooze!

Stop, stop, said Magnus Maharba; you are too much excited. You know that we must do justly, and observe the covenant of the fathers. I have but very little hope that the nobles and princes of the Dragon will accept my offer. Perhaps I shall not succeed with the people of a single province. But if they should return at my invitation, their rights must be respected. And after they have submitted to my authority, if they should still wish to honor and support the Black Dragon, subject to the laws of the country, we cannot force them to banish him from their midst. But I shall do my best to persuade them, and will give them almost any favor they ask, if they will abandon him. As to giving up Fredeema to the Dragon, if he should insist upon his claim, leave that to me. I will endeavor to pacify him with a ransom. Trouble not yourself and Fredeema with useless fears of what will probably never happen. If it should, unfortunately, become necessary, in accordance with the original bond, to unite her with one for whom she has no affection, I will take care that she is treated with every respect. She shall never, while I live, be forced to occupy the position of a menial. And she shall be allowed to spend the greater portion of every year on her favorite northern hills. Your daughter, I am sure, will always be ready, as I am, to make a sacrifice of her own private feelings, when necessary for the salvation of her country.

Then Fredeema could no longer contain herself, and she began to cry and sob bitterly. Clinging closely to her father, and leaning her head upon his shoulder, she trembled in every limb, as an aspen leaf trembles in the wind. And when she had partly recovered herself, she said, What is this that the king has done? For the king has put my life in jeopardy, and my enemies will now arise and combine for my destruction, and with their flattering words they will deceive the king, and as soon as they have made their peace with him, they will persecute me more than ever, and the poor innocent Kushans will be trodden to the dust, and hunted and killed upon the mountains and in the valleys, and in the caves where they have hid themselves. Oh, how can I endure to witness the sufferings of this kind, affectionate people? For they are to me as own brothers and sisters, and except deliverance be granted them, let the king know assuredly that I shall die with them, and my presence shall never more be a trouble to the king or to his people, and my name shall perish and be forgotten from among the inhabitants of this land. And she wrung her hands for the bitter grief and anguish of her soul.

Then the king was troubled, and he wept, and said to her father, Comfort the maiden, and pacify her, and doubt not that all will yet be well. So they bid her dry her tears, and her father told her he was pretty sure the Dragonians would reject the king's proposal. Her time of trial would be but for a few weeks, and then her sorrows would all be over; the Black Dragon would perish and sink to oblivion, the captives be delivered from their bonds, and all the people would hail her as the happy queen of a new and better age. But Fredeema could not hush her crying, and she besought 'the king that he would let her retire to the forests and compose herself, and remain there till the hundred days were past. To this the king would not consent, for he said, She will lose her reason if left alone with this anxiety preying upon her. He feared also that she might, in some rash moment of despair and bitterness, escape from the country and fly to other climes, and so fulfill the word she had spoken, that he and his people should see her no more. He kept her therefore in the palace, carefully watched and guarded, and he gave her the best room, and invited her father and friends to visit her every day, that they might soothe and encourage her. Notwithstanding all their efforts to make her happy, they could not restore her to her natural buoyancy. For Fredeema felt that she was a prisoner, and that she was still in danger of a fate worse than death, and that there was no certainty of relief for the captives over whose bondage she mourned. Often in the night she would wake from startling dreams, her heart throbbing convulsively. And every day she listened with intense interest to the rumors, whether of peace or war, that came from Sunland, hoping, yet scarcely daring to believe, that the Dragon would persist in his folly till his day of grace was past. Sometimes, when walking in the palace grounds, she would reflect bitterly on the conduct of the king, saying that he was unjust, and that he had no right to offer the Kushans as a bribe to win back the Dragonians. She could not understand the old covenants, nor the king's explanation of them; for she said if the covenants were for upholding injustice they were an abhorrence to the God of heaven, as much as they were to her. And further, she did not believe that a robber could acquire the right to rob by making a covenant with any body except the party to be robbed; and it was not pretended that the Kushans had consented to any of the covenants quoted by the king in justification of the Dragon's authority to oppress and injure them. As for herself, she deemed it a gross outrage for her father or any one else to make covenants or alliances for her against her will; and she called upon all the winged angels to lend their pinions and bear her to some other sphere, if there should ever be an attempt to force her into the Dragon's arms.

But when the Dragonians heard of the king's offer and threatening they derided them, and said, We have but to hold fast and be firm a little longer, and the victory is ours. And the king sent again for his officers, and bade them put their armies in motion, and march directly against the capital and palace of the Dragon. And Duke Burningbrand was commissioned to lead the way. And when he had reached the Rapidknocking river, and crossed over to the other side, he saw before him a high hill, and around it a great and strong wall. And when he drew near, it became a wall of fire, and belched forth showers of death-dealing missiles among his warriors. And many of them fell dead upon the plain, and they retreated once and again before the fiery ruin. And Horntosser begged of Burningbrand that he would keep away from the wall, for he was frightened at the numbers of the slain. But Burningbrand would not listen, for he said they must gain possession of the hill, cost what it might. So he waved aloft his flaming brand in presence of his whole army for the third time, and they rushed forward, and the Dragonians mowed them down as before, and piled the plain with the dead and dying, even ten thousand men. And Burningbrand had yet four score and ten thousand warriors left; and after the sun went down he gathered his dukes and chiefs in council, and told them that when the morning broke they must dash the remnant of their army once more upon the wall, if peradventure they might take it. And all the chiefs began to murmur, for they said, Why should we repeat this folly, and beat out the brains of the king's soldiers by throwing them against the wall, when we cannot reach the Dragonians that are behind it? Then Duke Burningbrand saw that all his supporters had failed him, and he was highly displeased, and ordered the army to be withdrawn to the northern bank of the river.

And there was great wailing and lamentation throughout Norland for the ten thousand warriors that had fallen before the fiery wall. And when the Dragon saw it, he grinned from ear to ear, and became more determined than ever not to submit to the king, or receive his offered pardon.

During the whole time of probation that had been given to the Black Dragon, the armies of the king were put to the worse before their enemies. For they could no longer hear the voice or receive the messages of Fredeema, and the power of her name as a watchword was lost. And some of the prophets that were of the Eradicators said that God was angry with them for offering to purchase the alliance and good-will of the Dragon with the toil and tears and life-blood of the Kushans, and that the stars in their courses were fighting against them, and that they never would be able to conquer their enemies until Fredeema was allowed to raise her banner over all the land for the protection of all the inhabitants thereof.

And Duke Rosycrown, who had been sent to watch the movements of Greatbrag beyond the Azure cliffs and Alligator mountains, resolved that the year should not pass without the glory of some victory for Historia to record in her diary. He therefore gathered together his bands that were scattered abroad, two score and ten legions, and marched toward Mothersboro, where Greatbrag and Breakingbridge and fifty legions of Dragonian warriors had pitched their tents and built their kitchens, and had sat down to eat and drink, and to make themselves comfortable for the winter. And when they heard that Rosycrown was advancing, they rose up in haste, and came out to give him battle on the banks of the Stonyfork river. And when thirty days of the Dozyember month had passed, and the aged year having laid himself down to die, sick and sad-hearted, unfolded his mantle to take one more sorrowful look at the morning sun, then the two armies began their deadly fray. And the Dragonians rushed upon Rosycrown in their fury, and he could not stand before them, and they swept down his legions by hundreds and thousands, even five thousand men; and they took two thousand captives and twenty great guns. Then Rosycrown fell back to the place he occupied at the opening of the fight, and there held fast his ground, and gathered his warriors around him, and bade them take heart once more, and remember that the darkest hour is just before the breaking dawn.

And so it proved; for the very next day the scale of battle turned, and the garlands of victory blossomed on the brow of Rosycrown. And he turned upon his enemies, and they fled before him, and he chased them to their camps, and drove them southward with a great slaughter.

CHAPTER XI.

LIBERATION OF THE KUSHANS.

IN the latter part of the closing month, when the end of the hundred days drew nigh, Fredeema grew more and more excitable, and her perpetual watching for the slightest whisper of doubt or hope had given her a wan cheek and a feverish pulse. She had carefully counted the weeks and the days, and now she began to count the hours. On the last day her anxiety was so intense that she would start at the rustling of a leaf, fancying that messengers had come from the Black Dragon to accept the king's offer. Finally, when she saw the sun go down, and close its glaring and bloodshot eye beneath the silken fringes of the twilight, and when the thought rushed upon her brain that the long agony was over, and that her destiny was safe, she broke forth into a convulsive shriek and swooned away. When she had recovered she found herself surrounded by her father and friends, who had come to congratulate her upon her good fortune, and the deliverance of the captives from their prison-house. And all that sympathized with her, in towns and cities, gathered together to watch the outgoing of the melancholy year, and to pray for the happy entrance of a better age.

But the night was dark and gloomy, and strange

noises were heard, and whistlings in the air, and a flapping of wings, as of demons enraged because their time was short. And the gloom rested upon the land till midnight. And when the Gate month, which opened into the new era, began to turn upon its hinges, and the great bells in the towers commenced their ringing, there came a soft white light that spread its radiance over the sky, and shone in at the windows, and with it a sweet melody as of distant warblings, and all that heard it said, It is the sound of the coming era! The angels are singing their old song of Peace on Earth, Good Will to Men! And the birds in their bowers thought the morning had come; and they too began to warble melodiously; and soft gales came up from Sunland, like the gales of Araby, laden with delicious perfumes; and all the people began to sing, and Fredeema sang, and the hours glided by before they were aware, and the morning broke.

And as the day advanced the people waited in anxious expectation for the king's decree which he had promised; and they said, Is not this the day for liberating the captives? And is not the day of grace for the Dragon past? Is not his doom to be pronounced this day? And some said, Magnus Maharba never yet broke his word; others said, he dare not banish the Dragon or deprive him of his servants; others, that it would not be just; others still, that it would be beyond the king's power to carry such a decree into execution.

Then the king gathered his ministers and scribes, and said, Ye know the warning that has been given; and now the word that has been spoken must be accomplished. So he inquired how many provinces there were that had sent no messengers to the great council. And they answered him, Ten. And he caused their names to be inserted in the decree which he had prepared. And the form of the writing was this:—

Whereas the Black Dragon, aided by treasonable and

wicked counselors, has made war against his king and country, and thereby forfeited all right to protection ;

And whereas a proclamation has been made giving warning and time for repentance, and offering pardon to all people and provinces in arms, on condition of their submission within the period of one hundred days, which hundred days have expired ;

Now, therefore, I, Magnus Maharba, king of the United Occident, do publish and declare, that all persons held captive within the following provinces, to wit, Virginland, North and South Carolers, Gorgeousland, Floweryglades, Islandbalmy, Fatherwater, Archangel, Louisland, and Takeusin, are henceforth and shall forever be Free; and their freedom shall be maintained by the national army and navy ; and they shall be employed to garrison forts, and to serve their country, and to labor for wages wherever they choose; and they shall have the right of self-defense if assailed by their enemies.

And the lords and counselors of the king approved the decree. And the minister that was over the king's treasury said, Let it be added that this act is performed in the name of Justice, and dedicated to Almighty God. And the king consented. And he signed the decree, he and Lord Seawarder, and they sealed it with the great seal, and sent it forth to be published throughout the land.

And the king called Fredeema, and told her that he had fulfilled his promise, and that she should never more be troubled or persecuted by the Black Dragon, but should be at liberty to roam at her pleasure through the whole country, Sunland as well as Norland, and to receive the love and homage of the inhabitants, and the grateful thanks of the liberated Kushans, and that her name should be inscribed upon all the king's banners. He added also the hope that she might one day become queen of all nations. Then Magnus Maharba took her hand and kissed it, and begged her forgiveness for whatever wrong he might have done her. And she kissed the king on both cheeks, and the king wept. For Fredeema being of heavenly origin, there was a current of celestial electricity that flowed from her lips as they touched the king's cheek, penetrating his whole frame, and kindling in his breast the same flame of impartial benevolence to all people with which she was herself inspired. And the king became as a new man, and he felt within himself that he had now received the true royal anointing, and from that hour he was ever ready and willing to lay down his life for the object of his devotion. And his lords, one after another, took the hand of Fredeema and kissed it. And they accompanied her out into the streets of the city, and a shout like the sound of mighty thunderings greeted her as she moved along. And the people strewed roses in her path ; and the Kushans gathered around her, and threw themselves at her feet, and wept for excess of joy.

And most wonderful it was to see how the whole Occident brightened with delight, as the echoes of the celestial music floated away on the wings of the wind to the distant mountains, and through the valleys and forests, and where the rejoicing rivers went pouring their crystal floods into the sea. And the evergreens opened their branches lovingly to the gales that kissed them as they went past ; and the icicles that hung around the Whitened Top of Mount Aguecheek softened into tears of tenderness ; and all along the Rocky crest that overlooks the Peaceful Sea, the eagles were out on poised wing, surveying the new beauties of the world beneath them ; and the clouds hung out their loveliest banners of red, white, and blue all over the sky ; and the oceans sent off their warm currents to melt the icebergs, and to sweep around the islands and the Great Orient, and to roll up their waves over the Barbarous shores of Kusha, and the burning sands of Ophir, and the green deltas of the Floweryland, and to wash out the foot-prints and the bloodstains which the Black Dragon and his father had left behind them in every country where they had had their habitation.

CHAPTER XII.

OPENING OF THE FATHERWATER.

ATHER than break the thread of my narrative in the east, I thought it better to be somewhat tardy in seizing the string of occurrences that happened in the west. That line I now take up.

Soon after the Dragon commenced his war, there was a mighty commotion in the granite hills where the Fatherwater has his sources, and in the wide and fertile plains through which they flow. For the Dragon had thrown an iron chain across the channel of communication, and would no longer allow the northern canoes and trading-boats to go up and down as aforetime. For the branches of the Fatherwater are spread over the central regions of the Occident as the branches of a tree spread through the air; and as the birds and squirrels are alarmed when they see a serpent twining around the trunk below them, so were the dwellers upon the western waters filled with consternation when they found the Dragon was throwing his coils across the great river and binding it with chains of iron, that he might make it a slave and a bondman, even as he had made the Kushans. And the people were roused, and poured down from their hills like torrents in the spring-time; and they said, Wherever our streamlets go, there will we go, and there shall be no chains upon our waters, from the Thousand Lakes, where our Minieshooters hunt the wildfowl, to the Great Basin of the Mixingcan, where the waters meet and mingle with the sea.

And there dwelt among the hunters of that region a tough and stubborn warrior whom they called Granite; and he was dressing the skins of wild beasts that had been killed in the mountains when he heard the tumult and murmuring of the people. And when they told him of the insult to the Fatherwater, he sent and offered his services to Samuncle. And Samuncle spoke for him to the king, and the king sent him a commission to cut a path down the Fatherwater and open the channel, so that the ships of the Admirable Fairygift, which lay in the Great Basin, might have a free passage up and down the stream.

Then Duke Granite gathered a great host of the Hillannoyers, and the Hieaways, and the Wisecounselors, and the Militiagunners, and the Minieshooters, and he marched them down to the border of Sunland, and made preparations to advance upon Mummyface and Wickedburg, two great cities that lay lower down on the banks of the Fatherwater.

And there came up from the south a warrior that would not enter into the counsels of the Dragonians, whose name was Sureman, and he joined himself to the king's armies, and was sent out to fight by the side of Duke Granite. And because of the greatness of the burden that rested upon the shoulders of these two chieftains, the spirits of two old warriors that had left the planet came back and entered into them, and possessed them, and made them strong for battle. And they came to them in dreams of the night, and infused into them a portion of their own qualities. And he that took possession of Duke Sureman was once a famous chief in the Occident, and was called Tecumseh; while the mentor that inspirited Duke Granite was an ancient hero by the name of Ulysses, that formerly dwelt in the Orient.

And Duke Granite became wise and cautious, and he would not move down the Fatherwater until he had secured the country on his left and right, so that the enemy could not come in behind him. Now there were two large and very crooked streams that rose in the Alligator mountains, and ran up towards Norland, as if they wished to enter the purer regions where Fredeema resided. And they went winding along side by side, very near each other, for a long distance, until they reached the Higherwater river, which, being a stronger stream, overpowered them, and turned them back into the Fatherwater, near the southernmost point of Norland, at a place where perpetual clouds of Egyptian darkness obscure the vision of the inhabitants. And the people who lived on the banks of these rivers, when they saw how lovingly they clung together in their course, said, These are twin brothers; and they called them Twin Seas. The northern stream was also known by the vulgar name of Cumberground. And when Duke Granite perceived that the Twinsea country was the key of the Fatherwater valley, and saw the desperate efforts that were made by the Dragonians to hold it for their battleground, he determined that his first fighting should be there. So he sent up Rightfoot, the commander of his ships, to storm the strongholds of the Twinsea which lay on his right. After these had been taken, Duke Granite moved forward with his footmen that were left, and marching to the Cumberground, which lay on his left hand, he surrounded the castle of Dawningsun, where a great army of Dragonians were gathered. And the Dragonian commander, Duke Flyingthief, assayed to fight, but the northern mountaineers overpowered him, and mounted his bulwarks, and cut down the boldest of his warriors, and pressed them sorely till nightfall. And when Flyingthief saw that the battle had gone against him, and that he and his legions must become captives on the morrow, he thought of all his thefts and his robberies which he had committed, and he was afraid to surrender himself to the king, lest he should be treated like a malefactor as he was, and be hung up by the neck. So he called his lieutenant, and gave him his plumes and his epaulets, and placed him in his stead, and instructed him what to do on the morrow. And when he had put all things in order, he rose up and took his Pillow under his arm, and fled, and made his escape in the darkness of the night, and was heard of no more.

And the next day was the day of the Sun, which was a sacred day, and when the morning broke, and Dawningsun castle began to glitter in the golden light, the lieutenant hastened to make his submission, and to deliver into the hands of the victor all his warriors that remained alive. And they counted the number of the captives, and found them to be thirteen thousand men.

Then the Granite Duke turned his face again to the west, and took up his line of march for the Fatherwater. But when he had crossed the Twinsea, he found Duke Prettyguard with a great army in his front near a temple that was known as the Silent Church. And the two armies joined battle, and they fought through two days, which were the days of the Sun and Moon, and then rested, because the place was so thickly covered with piles of dead and dying that they could no longer move over the ground. And they counted the slain and wounded of the king's army, and found the number was twice ten thousand; but the Dragonian dead were too numerous to count. And Prettyguard sent and besought Prince Jeffer that he would give him more warriors, lest the Granite Duke should seize upon the Fatherwater, and the great valley be forever lost. And great numbers were sent on to succor him; and he gathered them around the Corinthian columns that stood by the roadside on the way to Mummyface. But Duke Granite went forward and dispersed them; and he pressed on to Mummyface and took it. And he broke the chain that had been stretched across the Fatherwater, and destroyed the Dragon's water-rams that were swimming up and down the river, and butting at every thing that came in their way. Then he moved down the river to attack the Wicked city. And he found it was built high and strong, and terraced up from the water batteries to the summit; and its walls were full of dark holes, through which all manner of burning shells and iron balls were showered upon the ships that attempted to pass, and upon every enemy that ventured nigh. And one of the king's officers said, Let us make a new road for the Fatherwater, that he may flow to the sea by a straight channel, at a distance from the city, and be no longer defiled by contact with its polluted soil. So they dug a new channel broad and deep; but the Fatherwater was old and sluggish, and would not change his course to accommodate the new-fangled notions of either friends or foes.

The new era of Fredeema was now nigh at hand; but Duke Granite, like Rosycrown, was impatient for some victory before the old year should close. So he called Duke Sureman, in whom he reposed confidence, and sent him down the stream with orders to land his army on the eastern shore just above Wickedburg, and make an attack from the north. And Duke Sureman went and effected a landing as he was ordered. And three days before the new year he led his troops up to the walls of the city, and three thousand of his warriors were smitten down by the fiery besom that swept over and through them. And the ground where they trod was soft and miry, and at eventide the skies poured down their rainy torrents, and the wounded and dying sunk into the mire, and lay all night in pitiful helplessness and misery. And when the morning was come, Duke Sureman asked permission to bury his dead and bring away his wounded, which was granted. And when he had performed the last sad offices for his fallen comrades, he gathered the residue of his warriors, and placed them on board his vessels, and brought them back to their camping ground at Milkingpens.

After this failure Duke Granite began to devise new schemes for dislodging the Dragonians from the heights wherein they trusted. And he sent out his ships and his path-finders to penetrate the lakes and swamps and Roundabout bayus, on the right hand and on the left, if perchance they might find a way for his ships and army without passing under the walls of the city, but they could find none. And when he saw that the Gate month had come and gone, and the cool month of Febrifuge had also passed away, and the Marching month was now far advanced, he determined to send his war ships straight down the stream, and run them past the city under cover of a dark night, while he with his army marched down by a circuitous road on the west. And the ships and galleys were loosed from their moorings, and having put out their lights, they drifted slowly by the frowning battlements, and were not discovered till they were well-nigh beyond reach. Then the Dragonians lighted up their fires, and when they saw that the ships had gone by, their hill-tops resounded with rage, and they spit out after them streams of brimstone and fire, but all to no purpose. And Duke Granite brought his army around in safety, and having rejoined his vessels, he crossed over and came in behind the city, and besieged it. And he arrayed his guns against it, both from the land side and from the water, and rained upon it a storm of fire by day and by night. And Duke Peppercorn, who stood watching upon the walls, was indignant, and he prepared to defend himself to the last.

CHAPTER XIII.

SECOND INVASION OF NORLAND.

ING MAGNUS had now placed Duke Smoothbanks in charge of the lower regions of the Fatherwater, and Fairygift and Duepomp were over the ships. And because Horntosser was brave and daring, and was neither timorous like Micklemackle, nor inflexible like Burningbrand, he appointed him to be the leader of the eastern army, and told him to see if he could not pluck some of the feathers from the crest of Boldrobin. Then Horntosser put himself at the head of his warriors, and he sent off Duke Stonyman with four legions of horsemen to ride through Virginland, and to break down the bridges, and to let loose the channels of the water-floods, and to dash around the walls of Richmantown, and thus distract his enemies, while he with his whole army assailed them in front.

And on the second day of the Merry month the two armies met at Challengersville, and they had a hot and bloody battle of two days. On the first day of the fight some of the king's soldiers became confused, and saw spectres, and turned to fly. But as they fled Duke Bloodysickle placed himself in their path, brandishing his blade with one hand and holding a shortshooter in the other. And he drove them back, and they turned again upon the thundering legions of Stonyjack, and fought till the sun went down, and then the battle went on by moonlight. And a celestial watcher that was looking out from behind the silver lining of a cloud, when he saw upon the banners of Horntosser the name of the good Fredeema, and perceived that her cause was in danger, stepped down upon the plain where the fight was thickest, and threw a veil over the eyes of the men that followed Stonyjack. And they could not see the face of their leader distinctly, and he appeared to them like a Fredonian, and they leveled their longshooters and poured their fire upon him, and he fell down and died there. The next morning Boldrobin renewed the battle, and hurled his columns furiously against the Fredonian ranks. But Horntosser put forward the Burying Duke and the Burning Duke to resist him, and they overcame him, and covered the ground with his dead. And Burying Duke himself was slain. And there fell of the Dragonians eighteen thousand men; and of the Fredonians fifteen thousand.

And Horntosser was troubled because he could not hear the hoof-beats of Stonyman's horses, for they were now far away; and he said, Peradventure he has met with disaster. And while he waited and listened to catch the echo of his tramping, the clouds darkened, and a great storm of rain fell from the sky, and the Rapidrun and Rapidknocking rivers came thundering down from the mountains, on his right hand and on his left, and threatened to engulf him in their torrents. And when he saw the floods that were rising around him, he feared that his line of retreat would be cut off; so he withdrew his army, and they returned drooping and downcast to Fallenmouth and rested there.

Prince Jeffer was now elated, and he took counsel with the Dragon and said, This is the time for us to show our strength, for the coronation day of Fredeema is at hand, and the Normen are preparing to celebrate it with pomp and rejoicing such as was never known. For they have repudiated our alliance forever, and have already laid their plans for marrying Fredeema to the Prince Equality, who aspires to the sovereignty of the Orient; and when the union is effected, they together will rule the world. But let us pull out the pillars from under these fine air-castles, and put a stop to their coronation days, and turn their holidays and their rejoicings into mournful wailings and bitter tears. For we are well able to send our armies into Norland, and we will take possession of their king and his capital, and the cities and towns and strongholds shall open their gates at our approach, and all the gold and silver of the land shall be ours. For Prince Jeffer had secret agents in Brothercity and Gotham, and all the great towns, who stood waiting to open the gates; and also dangerous serpents, called Cobras, to be let loose upon the people of each city as fast as the Dragonian army came on.

And the Dragon approved of Prince Jeffer's plans, and they sent orders to Boldrobin to press forward, and they would give him as many soldiers as he needed. And they gathered their forces from the east and west, and the warriors were like locusts for multitude, and their shadow darkened the land. And they took up their line of march for the king's palace, but Horntosser stood in their path and prevented them. So they drew off toward the west, and went by the way of the mountains through the Laughing gap and Shiningdoor valley. And they crossed the Boundarymark river, and entered into the Penwood valleys, plundering and destroying as they went.

And the Normen saw that the time of their sore trial was come; for if they could not now beat back the victorious legions of Sunland, they must become their servants and serve them forever. And the Penwoodians sent in haste for helpers to all the region round about;

and the king called upon the rulers of the provinces to lend their aid and roll back the tide of invasion. And he sent off orders to his ships and warriors that were upon the eastern shore to move up the rivers and attack the Dragon in his rear. Then Jeffer was greatly alarmed, and sent off in haste to call back Boldrobin, but it was too late, for he was now far up in the Penwood hills.

And seven days before coronation day the king sent for Duke Honeywater, and gave him command of the armies, and charged him to move warily, and to bring Boldrobin into his snare, and by no means suffer him to escape and return to his master. And Duke Honeywater perceived that the struggle would be desperate and bloody; and he selected the valley of Deathsburg for his battle-field, and marshaled his hosts on Sepulchre hill, south of the city, and gave orders to his chiefs that if they saw any warrior turn his back to the foe, the penalty should be instant death. And Boldrobin, seeing the place he had selected, made his way to the same spot, and took possession of the hills on the north, and the Oaken ridges on the west, whose evening shadows threw a Classic beauty over the peaceful vale. And thither he brought his infantry, and his cavalry, and his artillery, a hundred and fifty great guns, and filled the woods with his warlike array.

And on the first day of the month Julius the battle began. For Boldrobin was anxious to fight before the troops of Honeywater had all come up; so he hasted and put forward Duke Earlystart, who fell heavily upon the Fredonian bands that were in advance of the rest, and captured about three thousand men. The next day the contest was renewed with still greater fury, and the cannon poured their iron storm upon the Round tops and Granite spurs of Sepulchre hill, and tore through the woody thickets of Wolves' mountain; and the artillery of the Normen peeled and splintered the ancient Oaks beneath which the Dragonians had taken shelter. And the dukes of Boldrobin, who had led the assault upon Sepulchre hill, returned to their chief when the sun went down, to consult and to receive orders for the morrow. For all knew that the next day would be the turning point of victory or defeat, and as this battle went, so they believed would turn the fortunes of the war.

And about midnight the Black Dragon, having heard of the fighting, and being roused to an unwonted pitch of excitement, left his palace, and glided along in the silence of the night until he reached the camp of his defenders; and he infused into the officers and soldiers all the virus of his nature, and mingling with the ranks, he breathed upon them his poisonous and intoxicating breath, until their eyes glistened like demons, and their veins throbbed with the heat of an unearthly fire. And the maddening vapor that shot from his nostrils filled the tent where Boldrobin and his dukes were drinking wine, inspiring them with the lust of vengeance. And Duke Yellwell raised his hand and swore with a bloody oath that on the morrow he would cut his way into the heart of the Fredonian army, or into the infernal regions. And the rest applauded him, and shouted Amen.

With the dawn of day the desperate struggle once more began. And Boldrobin directed Yellwell to attack and break the right wing of the Fredonian army, and thus prepare the way for the overwhelming assault which he had reserved for the centre. But Yellwell did not succeed, and after two thousand of his warriors had been smitten down to the ground, he sullenly gathered up the remnant and withdrew. The clangor of battle now ceased, and all was calm and quiet as a summer sea. But Boldrobin was secretly conveying his great guns around through the forest from the north to the west, where he expected to make his victory sure. And the Normen were joyous and light of heart, for they had no thought of the terrible storm that was to fall upon them ere the day closed. And they gathered around their camp-fires, and breakfasted, and sat down upon the grass, and made themselves merry, and sang songs. And the words which they sang were these: —

> "Ossamie's body lies mouldering in the grave,
> His soul is marching on.
>
> "Ossamie 's a soldier in the army of the Lord,
> His soul is marching on.
>
> "Ossamie's knapsack is strapped upon his back,
> His soul is marching on.
>
> "Ossamie's musket goes firing away,
> His soul is marching on.
>
> "Ossamie's pet lambs will meet him on the way,
> As they go marching on.
>
> "Now three cheers for Samuncle and Fredeema,
> As we go marching on."

The songs had died away, and the midday hours went peacefully by, until the bells in the tower of Deathsburg struck three, when suddenly the Oaken hills were all aflame, and shot and shell began to scream through the air, and the whole atmosphere was filled with flying missiles, bearing death on their wings and sweeping through the camp of the Normen. And they started up in terror, and their columns reeled and rocked beneath the overwhelming tempest, from which there was no escape. Under the sheet of hail that flew high above his head, Duke Highland was seen careering across the valley, followed closely by Longstep and the heavy battalions of Duke Steadyarm. And when they had reached the foot of Sepulchre hill, on which Duke Honeywater was encamped, there was a lull in the firing of the artillery, and lo! the Dragonians were ascending the hill-side, and advancing with flying banners to the charge. At this instant a shadow seemed to pass over the sun, and the Normen looked up and saw a towering form, with a dim outline, having the appearance of a thin light cloud, and shaped after the similitude of a man, but of colossal magnitude. Its feet appeared to rest upon the nation's capital, while its head extended up into the blue, and was surrounded with a halo of wondrous beauty. Down its breast flowed a long silvery beard. Its long and bony right arm, through which the sun's rays shone feebly, was stretched out towards the north, and held in its grasp the resemblance of a soldier's musket, from the end of which flowed a zigzag stream of electricity, pointing downwards, like a bayonet, in the direction of the Dragonian host. The left arm extended away to the southwest, pointing with a long pole, scarcely discernible, toward the lofty spires of the Wicked city, that lay on the banks of the Fatherwater. For a moment the soldiers stood gazing in wonder at this strange spectacle; then two or three cried out simultaneously, It is the ghost of Ossamie, with his musket and his pike! And the word flew from rank to rank, and soon a shout for Ossamie and Fredeema tore the welkin like the bursting of a thousand thunders. And the hearts of the warriors grew firm as adamant, and the electric current ran along their nerves, hardening them into steel. And they fixed every man his bayonet, in like manner as they had seen upon the sky, and dashed against their enemies with a fury that nothing could resist. Down went horse and rider; down went arms and banners. The legions of Steadyarm wavered for a moment, and then dropped on their knees, while the victors swept over them, and rolled through the valley, as the surges of the ocean roll when tide and tempest both press them on. And Boldrobin, when he saw the magnitude of his disaster, hastened and got him up into the mountains, and gathered the remnants of his army, and slunk away with his master the Dragon to the place from whence they came.

And the same day Duke Peppercorn came out from the walls of Wickedburg, and presented himself to Duke Granite. And he gave him the key of the city, and surrendered his warriors, thirty thousand in number, and two hundred great guns with which to salute the starry banner of Fredeema on the coronation morrow.

CHAPTER XIV.

DIABOLIAN METHODS OF WARFARE.

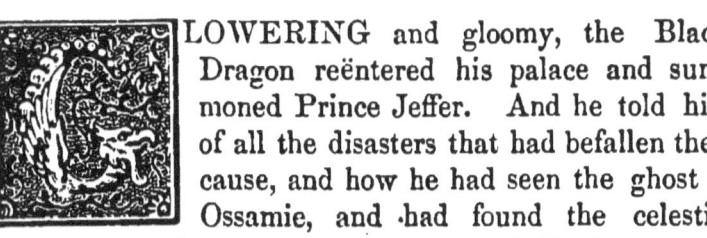LOWERING and gloomy, the Black Dragon reëntered his palace and summoned Prince Jeffer. And he told him of all the disasters that had befallen their cause, and how he had seen the ghost of Ossamie, and had found the celestial warders hovering round the banners of Fredeema, and that he deemed it useless to carry on the war in human wise any longer. He then proposed to telegraph to his father, who lived in the other planet that was lower down, and request him to give them aid. But for this purpose it would be necessary that Prince Jeffer should give himself up, and also his principal chieftains, to be wholly under his father's control; and they must allow the messengers of his father to enter into them, and make them the instruments of their will, to work out their objects in their own way. And all the instruments which his father might use to carry out his purposes must bind themselves by a firm obligation never to desert or renounce his service, but to obey him in all things and always. And Prince Jeffer counseled with Lord Judas and his other advisers, who were at first loath to bind themselves, but finally consented. Then they sent a telegram to the Red Dragon of Tophet, by means of the secret wires that united the two planets. And the

heart of the Red Dragon was moved with compassion for the sufferings of his son, and he sent off speedily a legion of malignant spirits to render to the earth-dwellers the service and assistance they needed. And they came by night, and were introduced to Prince Jeffer and his ministers; and when they had consulted and arranged their plans to mutual satisfaction, they divided themselves into bands, and went out to select their instruments. And it was agreed that some of them should enter into the Gothamites, and inaugurate a pandemonium in their city; others were to visit foreign countries and gather up dead men's clothes, and all sorts of plagues and poisons, and bring them over and scatter them abroad to destroy the inhabitants of the land; others were to poison the waters and burn the cities; and some were to proceed to Snowland, and feigning themselves to be messengers of peace, carry on the war by means of spies and murderers, who could strike in secret. And the most desperate of them were provided with infernal machines, by which they might destroy the king in his palace and his counselors in their bed-chambers. The chief of these was Guyfawkes, a demon who in a former age undertook to blow up the parliament of Bullia with his diabolical contrivances, but failed; he had now grown wiser in his craft, and was anxious to try his hand once more.

The first exhibition of the new mode of warfare was made in Gotham, upon which a squadron of evil spirits made their descent about the middle of the month of Julius. And the city was suddenly filled with Cobras hissing out their venom; and many of the Greenislers were bitten by them, and those that were bitten went mad, and ran hither and thither, burning houses and stoning the watchers of the city. And whenever they saw any of the Kushans they gave chase, and stoned them with stones, and beat them with clubs, and hung them up in the streets, and hacked and hewed them in pieces and burned them. And the chief ruler, whose name was Goodseemer, spoke kindly to the demoniacs and comforted them; and they shouted for Goodseemer and Boldrobin, and for Prince Jeffer and the Dragon, and their riotings and shoutings resounded through the city for three days. And when the king's officers were aware of it, they sent their armed bands to assist the watchers, and they slew and dispersed the men into whom the fiends had entered, and recovered the city, that it might again become a safe abode for human inhabitants.

And they that came up from the lower planet brought with them patterns of the prisons and templehouses in Hellham, where the Red Dragon resided. And there was a famous temple that stood on the shore called Nastrond, which is by interpretation Deathstrand, the walls of which were built of adders. The faces of these serpents were turned inward, and from their mouths issued streams of poison, forming a river that flowed through the vast structure. Queen Hela was the goddess that presided over it, and watched the prisoners sent to her for safe-keeping. The throne upon which she sat was Anguish; her table was Famine; her attendants were Expectation and Delay; her bed was Pain; she was livid and ghastly, and her very looks inspired horror. And the Red Dragon had given strict charge to Roughwind and Worstofall, two of his most skillful demons, that they should construct for him a temple in Sunland on the same plan, so far as practicable, with what materials they could find in the country, and that they should fill it with Fredonians, of whom one hundred were to be sacrificed every day.

And Roughwind and Worstofall, after consulting with Prince Jeffer, selected from his army two Dragonians that were admirably adapted to their purpose, one of whom was a general and the other a physician. And the demons took possession of their bodies and spirits, and infused themselves into their nature until possessor and possessed became one and the same being. And they made their first experiments under Prince Jeffer's own eye, at Richmantown, where they fitted up a Libertypen and Thunderhouse, and filled them with victims for sacrifice. But when the Black Dragon had examined the buildings he was dissatisfied, for he said they were scarcely equal, as torture-houses, to the dungeons for the Kushans which were built by their own people. Then Prince Jeffer advised with the demons, and they selected a place called Deadmansville, on the banks of Deathstream, where they thought they could produce a facsimile of Hela's own palace. So Roughwind marked out his ground, and drew his dead-line, and collected all the adders and rattlesnakes he could find, and built them up into the wall, with their faces looking inward, so that they might pour their venom upon the wretches congregated within. And he had hounds like the hounds of Hela barking round about, ready to seize and tear any that should attempt to escape.

And when Roughwind had completed the wall, he looked upon it with a delighted countenance, and laughed for joy, and said he would be of more service to Prince Jeffer than all the armies of Boldrobin. And they caught thirty thousand Fredonians and drove them into the enclosure, and Roughwind stripped them of their clothing, and Worstofall, who was the doctor, took charge of their food and medicine. So he gave them starvation for their meat, and poison for their drink. And the poison went down into their blood, and filled them with putrid sores, and they lay rotting in filth and vermin; and the stench spread over the whole region, and was borne on the winds till it reached the northern hills and entered the nostrils of Samuncle. And Worstofall mingled with his medicines some secret charm, by which he drew out the flesh from under the skin of his prisoners, so that the bones hung loosely as in a bag, and they moved and tottered in a manner that was horrible to behold. And the doctor would make the skeletons get up and dance before him for his amusement; and when they could not rise he would threaten them with new torments until they did. And the poor creatures became delirious, and they fought with each other, and desired to die, but could not, for Worstofall was careful to preserve their lives until the time for sacrificing them to his master. The number that he sacrificed was fifteen thousand, and the other fifteen thousand he kept alive as subjects for his experiments.

And the demons that went into Snowland took possession of Sandadder and Claycobra, and other serpentine natures, and they sent off their emissaries to break open the gold vaults in the Greenhills, and to burn the city of Gotham with fire, and to capture Shipcargo and Bisontown and Swinecity, and to cut a path through the midst of King Magnus' dominions, and sever the west from the east. And a host of ruffians were stirred up throughout Norland, and they appointed Vandalhammer, and Swingpendulum, and Longcobra for their leaders, and gathered great store of arms, and uttered swelling and towering words, and imagined that with their new helpers they would be able to depose the king, and establish a Dragonian dynasty whose reign should be perpetual.

And when the king and his counselors and the wise men of the land saw the blood and carnage, and the black thunder-clouds gathering on all sides, and perceived also that the princes and chieftains of Bullia and Gallia were in secret league with the Demonians, and when they heard the wailings of the wives and mothers of those that were pent up in Deadmansville, they were filled with bitterness, and groaned beneath the burden of their responsibilities. And one of the wise men of Gotham, he that was called Tribunosopher, wrote to the king and told him that the people could no longer endure their sorrows, and that he must in some way endeavor to make peace with the Dragon before it should be worse with them than it was then. He therefore advised the king that by way of showing the Dragon due honor and respect, he should build for him a bridge covered with gold, and invite him to walk away upon it, and pass over to some other shore; and when he had gone over, the bridge should be broken up, and the gold given to him by weight, according to the royal standard, twenty thousand shekels twenty thousand times told. But the proposal failed to indicate a spot where the other end of the bridge might rest, and the king knew that the Black Dragon was too sagacious to march off into the sea without being sure of obtaining a solid footing in some other region. Besides, he thought the Dragon had cost the country enough already, without offering him any further bounties.

And Sandadder and his associates, who were full of subtlety, wrote to the Tribunosopher to intercede for them, and procure them an audience with the king. And they invited him to visit them in Snowland to help forward the work of peace and compromise, so that all might be harmonious as before; for they knew that being an honest man he was unsuspicious of guile in others, and therefore would be the more easily entangled in their snares. For being anxious that every thing in the universe should be good and pleasant, and full of benevolence like himself, he was loath to believe that evil existed in any world except where he saw it with his eyes; and he could not be persuaded that the Black Dragon had a father, or that there was any Red Dragon, who lived in a lower sphere and sent out his emissaries on errands of mischief. He therefore did not hesitate to accept the invitation of the Diabolians, and after obtaining permission from the king, he went out to visit them. They, supposing the hour of the nation's agony was nigh, had seated themselves upon the brink of the Nighagony cataract, and were delighting themselves with its images of destruction. And when they saw the Tribunosopher approaching they smiled upon him agreeably, and he was pleased with their smooth words. But the king was anxious for him, fearing lest he might be unwary, and become a victim to their duplicity. So he sent a messenger to put an end to the conference, and thus the philosopher escaped and returned in safety to his home. And he continued to do the king good service; and he spoke to the people words of wisdom, and encouraged them to be strong for the war, until the Black Dragon should consent to quit the country.

But the king and Fredeema had made up their minds that whatever distress might betide, no further concession or compromise should be offered to the Black Dragon, nor would they furnish a single silverling either to bridge the mortification of his departure, or to build a monument for his grave.

CHAPTER XV.

TRIUMPH OF THE FREDONIAN ARMS.

ETERMINED at last to crush out the life of the Dragon, and wipe him from the face of the planet or die in the attempt, King Magnus addressed himself to the war with renewed intensity of purpose. And among all his generals he found none equal to Duke Granite; for although there were many loftier and more majestic warriors in his service, and those who could fight better in the beginning of a battle, there was no one who stood so erect in the end. For he was like a rock in the ocean, that looks all the fresher and fairer for the surges that sweep over it. And the king sent for him to come and fight Boldrobin, whom his other generals had allowed to slip through their fingers and escape, after they had conquered him twice.

But before he left the regions of the Fatherwater, Duke Granite cleared the channel of the Twinsea all the way up to the mountains; and he drove the Dragonians out of Shadowynook, and chased them up to the top of Lookover mountain, where they defied him to reach them. And Horntosser was sent to assail them and drive them down. And he went up and fought them on the summit, for it was above the clouds; and there he found Greatbrag, and he struck him with the tip of his horn, and tossed him down the precipices. And he went rolling over and over, until at last he fell into the Chickenmocking brook, which served to cool his ardor somewhat, and to diminish his brag and bluster. And Breakingbridge was with him, and he also broke down and fell into the stream. And Duke Granite left Sureman and Horntosser to look after the broken fragments of Greatbrag's army, while he went to see the king.

And the king received him with honor, and made him chief captain of all his armies, east, west, north and south; and he called upon Samuncle for five hundred legions more of fresh warriors. And he issued his summons to the Kushans, bidding them rally under the Fredonian flag, and fight for themselves and for their country. And they came by hundreds and by thousands, wherever the king's invitation reached them, and eagerly joined the ranks of their deliverers. And the great guns of Samuncle began to thunder and lighten all round the horizon. And Duke Killmore waved his cimeter along the eastern coast, and Dullgreen, a son of the ocean, was sent with ships and floating towers to aid him in recovering Stonepile castle, and in the capture of Churlstown, the original den where the rattlesnakes were hatched. And they sent into the city their fiery messengers, and their swamp-angels, and battered down the walls of Stonepile, and made it a ruin; but they dared not enter it for fear of the serpents that were concealed amongst the rocks and rubbish.

And when the spring opened, Duke Granite took up the gauntlet that Boldrobin had thrown down, and marched along the line of advance that Doitwell and Micklemackle, Burningbrand, Horntosser, and Honeywater had been unable to follow. And he took the line in his hand, and told the king he should not let go until he reached the end of it, if it took him all summer. And he invited Fredeema to accompany the army; so she went along with them. And when he had come to the Wildwoods that lay beyond the Rapidrun river, he found the woods filled with the warriors of Boldrobin, a new and mighty army, which their leader deemed invincible. And they fired upon the Fredonians from copse and thicket, and charged upon them, and fought fiercely for two days. And there were slain and wounded on each side about ten thousand men. And at night the Dragonians retired from the Wildwoods to the Spotwoods, where there were fine spots of open plain, convenient for fighting. And there the two armies again joined battle, and fought for six days longer. And with all his skill and prowess, and all the secret help the Dragon could render him, Boldrobin was unable to shake the rocky firmness of his antagonist. And Duke Granite pressed onward, and crossed the Chickenominous swamps, and sat down with his army to besiege the strongholds of Richmantown, in like manner as he had besieged and conquered Wickedburg.

And Fredeema was impatient, and she said, Let me go into the heart of Sunland, and call out the Kushans to fight for us, and we will have the speedier victory, and shall not have to bury so many of my father's soldiers, for it sickens me to see the slaughter. And after considering her request for a day and a night, he formed his plan, and sent her with an escort to Duke Sureman, who was fighting Stonyjohn in the Gorgeousland, and directed him to assist her, and to receive and encourage all the Kushans she might bring him. And Sureman closely scrutinized her credentials, for he was afraid she would give him trouble. But when he saw her queenly bearing, and how majestically she unfurled the tricolored banner, and how the warriors shouted as she passed before them, his admiration was kindled, and he offered to go wherever she would point the way. Then Fredeema cast her eye toward the eastern sea, and she told him that he must cut a swath through the whole breadth of the Dragon's dominions, and bear glad tidings of deliverance to the wasting skeletons in Deadmansville, and sweep along the ocean shore till he could join hands with his fellow-warriors at Richmantown. And Duke Sureman said, It is well; the deed is a desperate one, but it shall be done. And he lifted himself up to the occasion; and he took a hundred thousand warriors in his train, and began his march. And he went over the mountain ridges, driving the legions of Stonyjohn before him, and the ground shook beneath the tread of his warriors as if an earthquake had been passing. And Duke Bishoppolk, the great Dragonian soul-doctor, met them among the Pines of the mountains, and there he was slain. And when Stonyjohn could no longer stand in battle, Duke Knighthood, a furious and desperate warrior, in knightly armor, came out to meet them, and bar their entrance into the Gate city. And he fought three battles and was discomfited, and there fell of his warriors twenty thousand men. And he fell back chagrined and crestfallen, and left the spacious plains of Gorgeousland to the mercy of the conqueror. And when Duke Sureman had passed through the Gate city, he cut asunder his lines of connection with the west, and spread his wings for the ocean. And the eagle screamed, and Fredeema took her place in the van, and she put on her garment of red, white, and blue, and a crown was upon her head, and the drums and trumpets struck up their victorious anthems by her side. And the road she traveled was suddenly begemmed with buds and blossoms; and wherever she adventured to put the sole of her foot upon the ground, fresh blooming roses sprang up beneath it; and the spring flowers of the northern prairies spontaneously burst forth over all the savannas of Gorgeousland. And the Kushans came out to meet her with songs and dances; with their wives and little ones they crowded around her to kiss the fringes of her star-spangled robe; and neither threats nor entreaties could turn them back from following her. And when the Dragonians saw the crown that was upon her head they trembled and shrank from her gaze; and their dukes and princes could not find a single warrior that dare oppose the march of the victorious army so long as she was at its head. And the vipery walls of Deadmansville fell down, and Worstofall and his watchmen fled hither and thither to seek for hiding-places where they might not meet the glance of her eye.

And when Duke Sureman began to near the ocean, and the sound of his trumpeters rolled along the savannas that lay on the coast, Duke Hardihood, who stood sentinel in that quarter, lost his fortitude and his hardness, and his nerves grew limp and lax like a woman's, and he gathered up his legions by night, and fled for refuge to Churlstown. But the music and tramping of the Fredonian army followed him thither also; so he set fire to the city and ran for his life. And Fredeema entered the city and walked through the streets, and the men of Churlstown grew gentle, and came out to salute her; and when they saw her they were captivated with her loveliness, and took an oath that they would worship the Dragon no more.

And when the Dragon saw that Duke Granite had closely shut him up on one side, and that Sureman and Fredeema were pressing him hard on the other, and would soon cut off his only line of retreat, he began to perceive that his hour was at length come. And he rolled and writhed in agony, and the perspiration gushed out from beneath his glossy scales, and he could get no sleep at nights, and he had spasms and contortions that were dreadful to behold. Then Jeffer and Boldrobin, seeing how the glory of their idol was departed, concluded to leave him to his fate, and look only to the safety of themselves and their armies. And it was decided that Boldrobin should go out and give battle to Duke Granite, and if defeated they would then abandon the palace and capital, and make their way southward through the mountains. So Boldrobin went out to Hatchet brook, and there he met his conquerors, and they mowed down his warriors, and rode back and forth through their ranks, and slaughtered them with a great slaughter. And Duke Highland was slain, and Yellwell was surrounded and taken. And Boldrobin turned his face to the mountains, but the cavalry of Fleetsheriff were on his track, and he could turn neither to the right hand nor to the left. And when he saw the advancing army of Duke Granite closing around him, his judgment and his reason returned, and he raised the white banner and went out to meet his adversary. And he took off his helmet and plumes, and made his salutation, and presented his weapon to Duke Granite; and Duke Granite took him by the hand, and the hatchet was buried.

And there still remained Duke Stonyjohn and forty thousand Dragonian warriors watching on the banks of the Fearful river for the approach of Sureman and Fredeema. And hearing of the disaster of Boldrobin he turned himself to fly, but Duke Sureman stood in his path; and when he saw there was no escape, he also threw down his hatchet at the feet of the conqueror, and they buried it there. And the soldiers of the two armies became brothers, and danced together beneath the king's new banner, into the texture of which the name of Fredeema had been inwoven.

And the Dragon, when he found that Boldrobin and Stonyjohn had forsaken him, beat his forehead and lashed himself with his tail; and his attendants fled, thinking he would sting himself to death like a scorpion. And he disappeared from his palace in the night, gliding off into the woods to hide himself, and he returned to hold his court there no more. And the king went down to see what had become of him, and he found his palace empty. And he examined the dungeons and chains, and the instruments of torture which the grisly tyrant had left behind him; and he opened the gates of the Liberty-pens and Thunderhouses, and brought out the captives.

Nor was Prince Jeffer to be found at his old habitation; for on the day when Boldrobin presented himself to Duke Granite, which was a holy day, they brought the tidings to Jeffer, as he sat worshiping in a Dragonian temple, and he rose up hastily and fled. And he went swiftly toward the southern sea, hoping to find some Bullian vessel in which to make his escape. But he was hemmed in by the soldiers of the king who were everywhere scouring the country. And when he perceived the case he was in, and had come to the end of his wits, and knew not what further to do, he raised one last and piteous prayer to the father of the Black Dragon whose servant he had been; and the old deceiver compassionated him, and changed him into a woman, and clad her with female apparel, so that she might not be known. But he neglected to remove her sandals, which were strong and serviceable, and which she wished to retain. And one morning, as she was walking out with her milk-pail upon her arm, she saw that the grass was dewy, and raising her dress to keep it from getting wet, her sandals were discovered by some soldiers that were passing that way. And they apprehended her, and bade her confess to them who she was. And she would not answer, but told them they ought to be ashamed to make war upon women. But the soldiers would listen to no entreaties, and in spite of her struggles they carried her off to their officers, by whose orders she was lodged in a prison.

CHAPTER XVI

MARTYRDOM OF MAGNUS MAHARBA.

OTWITHSTANDING the Dragonian armies were now disbanded, and the conflict to all outward appearance closed, yet the demons still lingered to carry out their fiendish malevolence, being determined not to yield as long as there was a single instrument left to do their bidding. And Guyfawkes, the most crafty and daring of them all, entered into a Booth that was near a theatre, not far from the palace, and there he laid his plans for the king's destruction. For he had brought up with him from the other planet an arrow, whose point had been dipped in the water of death, and its shaft was winged with the feather of certainty. And he sought opportunity to dart it against the body of the king. And he consulted with the other emissaries of Prince Jeffer that were in Norland and Snowland, and those that were in Middleland, near to the royal city. And he selected for his co-workers Powerfulpain, and Hastywroth, and Sherat, and Childharold, and Secondarnold, and Mudpills, and Laughingfiend. And Sherat invited them nightly to banquet in a spacious cavern near the king's palace, where the Dragon was secreted. And there they concocted hellbroth and fed the Dragon, and nourished his hopes that he might yet be able to hurl Magnus Maharba from his throne

and get possession of the kingdom. And they made for themselves explosive machines and missiles of death, and sharpened their daggers, and assigned to each actor his part in the drama they were about to perform. For they purposed to destroy the king and his lords, and Duke Granite all at the same moment, so that they might rush into the palace amid the confusion and consternation of the people, and fix the Dragon so firmly upon the throne that he could not be displaced.

And while the enemies of the king were plotting his destruction, one of the heavenly watchers came to him in a vision of the night, and painted on his brain, as he was sleeping, a dismal picture of blood and horrors; and when he awoke the picture was still clear and distinct. And in the morning his friends came to visit him, and they saw that his face was pale, and the form of his visage disturbed. And he told them his dream, and how he had seen an ocean of blood, and himself swimming therein. And the watcher that painted the dream had whispered in his ear that the great drama was to close at the end of four years from the time it began; and that the ocean of blood was in requital of the wrongs done to the Kushans; and that for every drop drawn by the lash there must be another drawn by the sword; and whatever was wanting to make the recompense perfect must be paid by the blood of a costly sacrifice. And the king's advisers, after hearing it, went out and consulted together, and sought to understand the dream, but they could find none that was able to divine the interpretation. Yet they deemed it the harbinger of evil; and they placed a strong guard around the palace by way of precaution, and another to watch the king's person. And they computed the time of four years from the commencement of the war, when the king's flag was torn down from Stonepile castle, and they found the period would end on the fourteenth day of the Openrill month, which was the day of Goodsacrifice. And they said, Let us make it a glad and joyful day, and a day for the celebration of peace and victory, and for the unfurling of banners, and for orations and illuminations; and peradventure the shadow will pass off from the king's mind. And they craved permission of the king to unfurl the old banner from the summit of Stonepile castle on the anniversary of its first dishonor. And the king was pleased, and he gave command to his warriors, and on the evening of Goodsacrifice day the star-spangled banner once more waved over the ruins of the castle, and the cannon poured forth their joyful salute.

And the same evening the king was sitting in a play-house, where they had persuaded him to go that he might shake off the burden of his cares. And just as the roar of the guns around Stonepile castle proclaimed the closing of the great drama, Guyfawkes and the other demons who assisted him hasted to perform their parts in the concluding scene. And they crept stealthily into the play-house where the king had entered, and as the king leaned forward unsuspectingly to observe the acting of the players, the arrow that was pointed with death, and winged with the feather of certainty, struck him in the back of his head, and he fell to the floor unconscious. And Guyfawkes started up from behind the king, flourishing his dagger, and shouting in the ears of all the people that he had killed a tyrant. And he leaped upon the stage, and out at the door, and was gone. And the same hour of the night Powerfulpain entered the chamber of Lord Seawarder, who was lying on a sick-bed, and he smote him and would have killed him, but the celestial guardians threw their shields over him and warded off the blows.

And the king's servants removed him to a private chamber and laid him down to die. And his lords, and they that loved him, and Fredeema, stood around his bed, and watched him until the morning. And because his vitality was strong, the king lingered in his dying, and the body and spirit struggled in their unclasping. And when the sunlight looked in at the window the weary throbbing ceased; and the king gave up his ghost, and it became disentangled from its attachments, and floated upward to dwell with the immortals. And Fredeema put her lips to the king's clay, and kissed his cold face, and she said, Alas, alas, that thou shouldst die for me! For if thou hadst not pitied this sorrowful child, and taken her part when there was none else that could deliver her, thou mightest still have lived, powerful and honored among the kings of the earth, and my poor name would have perished from the memory of men. And she covered her face, and poured forth her anguish in a torrent of tears.

And a voice of wailing went up from the royal city, and it spread and increased in volume as it rolled over the land. And all the gay cities were suddenly draped in the weeds of mourning; and the sun grew dark and gloomy; and the warders of the sky stretched their clouds of crape over the pillars of the east and west; and a pall was spread over the mountain tops, and over the lowly vales, and all the trees of the forest were fringed with funereal tassels; and men spoke not for horror, and every pulse paused in its beating, as if the crack of doom had sounded from a clear sky.

And when the terror had abated, a cry of vengeance arose on the air, and the Dragon heard it in his hiding-place. And he at once comprehended that there was no den so dark, no gulf so deep, no mountain so high, as to give him a quiet resting-place on the planet where he had done this deed. So he put on darkness for his covering, and came out of his hole, and shrieked a wild shriek to summon the demons that should accompany him on his departure. And he raised up his lofty form, and spread his pinions for the home of his father; and the mold of oblivion settled on his wings, as they disappeared beneath the thunder-clouds that skirted his downward way.

And Samuncle sent out hunters to search for the men that had entertained the demons, and had been their instruments in the murder of the king. And when they had caught them, they hanged them up to die in the sight of the mourning and angry heavens. But they could not kill the demons that had instigated these wretches; for they had gone out of the men and abandoned them to their fate, as soon as they had no further service for them to perform.

Now there was in that country a massive and lofty column, on which it was the wont of Historia to record the names of departed heroes and statesmen, and all the great and good that were deserving of remembrance. It was pyramidal in form, and vast in dimensions, and the clouds rested on its summit. And after the multitudes had returned from viewing the king's corpse, they gathered around the monument to witness the inscribing of his name. And Historia took her longest ladder, and set it up against the side of the column, and they watched her as she ascended; and Fredeema climbed up after her to see where she would put the name of her favorite. And while she was passing over the spot where the names were most thickly written, the people gazed intently, expecting every moment that she would stop and begin. But she went on and on, until she had left the vast crowd of statesmen and warriors beneath her feet. And she passed the long line of kings, King Adam, and King Jeffer, and King Andrew, and King Adam ben Adam, who befriended Fredeema in her childhood, and Ossamie the Martyr, and all the philanthropists and martyrs that had given their lives for the welfare of their race. And when the people saw that she still kept ascending, they gave a loud shout, for they then understood that it was a great and noble king that had passed away from among them. Now there was written, far up and distinct from the rest, a single name, in large characters, yet scarcely visible for the distance; the name was

PATER PATRIAE.

And they watched Historia as she fixed her eye upon the spot; and Fredeema closely followed her. And when she had reached the place, she took from her girdle an iron style, and placed her hand on the rock to write, just beneath the solitary name. And while the multitude were shouting, and before the rock was pierced, Fredeema spoke and said, My sister, do you remember the four millions of liberated Kushans? And Historia dropped her eyes, and remained for a moment in thought, then stepped upon the next round, and placing her fingers just over the ancient letters, began to carve the rock with a clear bold stroke. And all the people were amazed and confounded, for it was a fixed belief of all the men of the Occident that no name could ever be written above that of the Father of his Country. But when Historia withdrew her hand, and they saw the name

MAGNUS MAHARBA,

and knew that it was engraved for all time, in characters enduring as the eternal hills, their minds were illuminated, and they saw with new eyes, and their shoutings were changed to tears of glad and wondering emotion, and they clasped their hands in prayer, and gave thanks to the God of heaven that they had been allowed to look upon the face of so noble a king and martyr, the deliverer and savior of his country.

And Samuncle and all the people embalmed the body of King Magnus Maharba, and laid it in a tomb; and his memory they embalmed in their affections. And the nations of the Orient mourned and lamented him; and the Victorious Queen of Bullia touched the harp of sorrow; and they called him by the name of Maharba the Good.

And King Andrew the Second reigned in his stead.

www.ingramcontent.com/pod-product-compliance
Lightning Source LLC
Chambersburg PA
CBHW020153170426
43199CB00010B/1015